Classical Music

LA

of

G000138797

OMNIBUS PRESS

Cover & Book designed by Chloë Alexander
Picture research by Graham Vickers & Nikki Lloyd

ISBN: 0-7119-8676-2
Order No: OP48312

Exclusive Distributors
Music Sales Limited
8/9 Frith Street
London W1D 3JB, UK.

Music Sales Corporation
257 Park Avenue South
New York, NY 10010, USA.

The Five Mile Press
22 Summit Road
Noble Park
Victoria 3174, Australia.

To the Music Trade only:
Music Sales Limited
8/9 Frith Street
London W1D 3JB, UK.

All location photos by Graham Vickers

Every effort has been made to trace the copyright
holders of the photographs in this book but one or
two were unreachable. We would be grateful if the
photographers concerned would contact us.

Printed in Malta by Interprint Limited

A catalogue record for this book is available from
the British Library.

Visit Omnibus Press on the web at
www.omnibuspress.com

Classical Music
LANDMARKS
of LONDON

Graham Vickers

OMNIBUS PRESS

Using This Book

- All landmarks included here are accessible by London Underground. Some are closer to the nearest Tube station than others, but usually the walk will be reasonably short. There are no maps included, and you are advised to take with you a reasonably detailed London street map, preferably one with a Tube journey planner included. If you are a visitor to London, most of the included landmarks are within the range of a one-day, four zone Travelcard that will let you make as many Tube (and bus) journeys as you have time for in 24 hours.

- Entries have been grouped by London postal district, which means that often several locations will be found in close proximity to one another, both in the book and in real life. The central London W1 district has the most entries.

- Each landmark has a current reference picture that makes identifying its location easy. Although it is hard to miss something as big as The Barbican Centre, some of the more obscure locations are much easier to find with the help of the picture.

Understandably, given London's history, a Landmark will often have been radically remodelled or demolished. Its site is still included if its story is considered to be of sufficient interest. Thomas Britton's famous house in Jerusalem Passage has been replaced several times over the centuries, but that does not make a visit to the present building with its commemorative plaque a waste of time. Unlike the small Santa Fe shop I once saw advertising its imminent conversion into the jail that once held Billy The Kid, London has no need to reinvent its past in a theatrical way. The pictures indicate what you are likely to find as well as what to look for.

The index at the back includes all of the musicians who, for whatever reason, made these landmarks famous, infamous or in some other way worth taking a look at. Enjoy!

Contents

- London is extraordinarily rich in classical music landmarks. In venues ranging from an early 18th century room above a Clerkenwell coal depot to the opulent setting of The Royal Albert Hall, fine music and its creators have always found a home in the capital. During the past three hundred years or so the city has been a magnet for nearly all of the great national and international composers, conductors and performers. For them London's cultural attraction must have been considerable, because in other ways the city proved itself almost comically inhospitable. For a long time this was largely due to its legendary susceptibility to fog – which was actually not fog at all but highly toxic air pollution. This, combined with a damp, chilly climate and a leaden diet could usually be depended upon to render all but the most robust visitor bedridden practically at once. Rossini was laid up for a week as

soon as he arrived at his London hotel, Chopin dubbed the climate "hellish" and Mozart's father wrote a letter of utter bewilderment about his encounter with a peculiarly British infirmity known as a cold. In fact most correspondence written by the great men of music to the folks back home dwelt not upon the cultural focus of their visit but upon their utter unpreparedness for London's yellow atmosphere, invisible sun, dank climate and depressing cooking. But still they came, and some of their fame rubbed off not just on the places where they performed or worked but also on the places where they lodged, lived or visited. Because in spite of the grand statues and official memorials, Handel still needed somewhere to hang his hat, Mozart's father had to find adequate accommodation for his remarkable offspring and Mendelssohn craved bread-and-butter-pudding which he would ask his landlady to leave as a nightcap for him after a concert. Such trivia form the sub-text of this little guide. Some of the landmarks included would still be buildings of great architectural interest even if we

knew nothing of their links with Rossini, Mahler or Chopin. Others are fairly anonymous places, worthy of attention just because of some chance but diverting association with this composer or that conductor.

The world may revere the great musicians for their exceptional qualities, but it is their unexceptional qualities that somehow make them more human. Although one or two of them suffered from impressive neuroses, most of them just had problems. Whether it is the composer of Siegfried waging a Wagnerian battle against the common cold, Strauss The Elder squabbling with a deficient hotelier or Delius demanding that all of the ticking clocks in Sir Henry Wood's house be silenced for the duration of this visit, there is something heartening about seeing celebrated men faring no better than the rest of us with everyday life in the big city. Here then are some of the London buildings once touched by the presence of the world's most memorable musicians who, by being there, helped to make those buildings memorable as well.

G.V.

- **THE LANGHAM HOTEL** 1C Portland Place, Regent Street (Tube: OXFORD CIRCUS). The present day Langham Hotel is now part of the Hilton chain. Prior to that and for many years it acted as a rambling annexe to the BBC's Broadcasting House situated diagonally opposite. But in its heyday the original Langham Hotel boasted many musicians and composers as guests – again, perhaps because of its proximity to the BBC and also to Queen's Hall (destroyed in the war and now replaced by another hotel). Queen's Hall was the place where most classical music recordings were made before the opening of Abbey Road Studios in 1931 (**see NW8**).

Built in 1864, The Langham was a favourite watering hole of **Sir Thomas Beecham** and **Sir Edward Elgar**. **Jean Sibelius** also stayed there on his last two visits to London. Previously Sibelius had boarded at a house near Campden Hill where he finished his String Quartet and apparently learned to enjoy the city. He later confessed to **Claude Debussy** that his own experience in London gave lie to the

Sir Thomas Beecham

widespread opinion that "Englishmen have no natural talent for music". Instead Sibelius concluded that although the English were very capable musicians, "in their splendid isolation they do not trouble to advertise themselves". His desertion of his boarding house for The Langham may have been influenced by a downstairs

The Langham was a favourite watering hole of Sir Thomas Beecham and Sir Edward Elgar

neighbour who was more than happy to advertise herself by tackling The Moonlight Sonata on an out-of-tune piano in a misjudged show of musical solidarity with the composer upstairs.

Leoš Janáček also chose The Langham for his only visit to Britain in the spring of 1926. Its proximity to Regent's Park and the London Zoo encouraged him to spend some time observing the monkeys and assiduously noting down the sounds they made. The results obviously pleased him because on his return to The Langham he seemed to find equal fascination in the speech patterns of the hotel's pageboy whose pronunciation of the word "yes" appeared to beguile him. We have no record of what questions Janáček may have asked to elicit so many affirmative answers, but by the time he checked out, he had twenty variants of that spoken word transcribed in his notebook. **Frederick Delius** stayed at The Langham for the duration of The Festival of 1929 and it was here that Augustus John sketched a well-known portrait of the Bradford-born composer. The sketch can now be seen at The Royal College of Music (**see SW7**). When **Antonin Dvořák** chose The Langham for one of his nine visits to London, he caused a mild Nabokovian stir by booking a double room for himself and his young daughter. However, he successfully persuaded the management that the arrangement was motivated purely by considerations of economy.

- - - Number **58 QUEEN ANNE STREET** (Tube: BOND STREET) is just one of several places where French composer, critic and conductor **Louis-Hector Berlioz** stayed when in London. The composer of *Symphonie Fantastique* and *Roméo et Juliette* always seemed vaguely unwelcome in his native France, an impression dating from the time he won the 1830 Prix de Rome at the Paris Conservatory, the conditions of which stipulated that he must immediately spend three years abroad. Since this coincided with his first major success – *Symphonie Fantastique* – the prize at once stifled his chances to cash in on his

newfound fame in France. Berlioz's final years too were marked by distinction in several foreign countries but something close to hostility at home. His stay at Queen Anne Street, which is celebrated with a blue plaque, took place in 1851 when he was in London representing France on the musical jury at The Great Exhibition. It was on this visit that Berlioz wrote his fulsome – indeed, almost hysterical – account of the seductiveness of the London season.

"'The London Season! The London Season!' is the cry of every Italian, French, Belgian, German, Bohemian, Hungarian, Swedish and English singer" he raved. "Just as the soldiers of Aeneas, when they boarded their ships shouted 'Italiam! Italiam!'" It seems Berlioz saw the London Season as such an intoxicating event partly because of the sheer amount of musical productions it staged and partly because of the

exceptional loyalty of London audiences. "Thanks to this immense consumption," he concluded, "all artists with genuine talent... are assured of work (in London). They are expected to return every year... it is assumed they will reappear, like the pigeons in North America." (This prompts the thought, are North American pigeons more likely to return than those of any other country? Perhaps Berlioz was thinking of swallows returning to Capistrano). Dubious avian similes aside, there is no doubting Berlioz's love affair with London and its audiences, which he saw as being faithful almost to the point of indiscrimination, ready to applaud and admire foreign artists "without perceiving the irreparable ravages of the years". Sadly his warmth was not always reciprocated, as this bracing assessment in the British journal Dramatic and Musical Review attests. "Berlioz, musically speaking, is a lunatic," it began, obviously not wanting to sugar-coat the matter, "a classical composer only in Paris, the great city of quacks". Going on to characterise Berlioz's music as being "simply and undisguisedly nonsense" the reviewer dismissed him as "a kind of orchestral Liszt, than which I could name nothing more intensely disagreeable". On the other hand the British musicologist **Sir Donald Tovey**, on first hearing Berlioz's *Les Troyens* said it is "one of the most gigantic and convincing masterpieces of music drama" although he added worriedly, "You never know where you are with Berlioz."

"Berlioz, musically speaking, is a lunatic"

Much of the east side of **MANDEVILLE PLACE** (tube: BOND STREET) has for many years been occupied by The Mandeville Hotel, a large Marylebone establishment located directly opposite Trinity College of Music. On the wall a blue plaque celebrates the 20-year residency of the composer **Francesco Paolo Tosti** in a house, number 12, on the site. Tosti was born in Ortona sul Mare, Italy in 1846 and was to die in Rome in 1916. In his late twenties he had arrived in London, a fashionable destination for European composers looking to build a career. Queen Victoria's love of music had helped to make the capital a highly welcoming city for top musicians and Tosti's gifts as a composer, pianist and tenor singer immediately made him a welcome addition to London society. In 1880 he decided to settle permanently in London having set up his famous singing classes that were attracting the children of the most exclusive elements of English society. Even Queen Victoria's own children attended Tosti's classes and he also acted as impresario for the monarch's numerous private concerts. Tosti taught at both the Royal College of Music and the Royal Academy of Music and wrote many songs that were to become popular in the Victorian music halls in the capital and throughout Britain. Among many honours bestowed, Tosti was made a Baronet in 1908 and only left his adopted city to return to Italy in the final years of his life.

Even Queen Victoria's own children attended Tosti's classes

Number **25 BROOK STREET** (Tube: BOND STREET) was the home of **George Frederic Handel** (a name with many variant spellings including Georg Friedrich Händel) for nearly 40 years. Handel was born

in Germany in 1685 and made his second trip to England in 1712. This visit was supposed to be temporary but Handel's second leave of absence from his German employer, the elector of Hanover George Louis, was extended indefinitely. Fêted by prominent members of both the English aristocracy and the intelligentsia, Handel was in no hurry to return to Germany and he eventually decided to settle in London permanently. After staying at various addresses, including one in the northwest district of Edgware, he put down roots here in Mayfair at 25 Brook Street for which premises he paid £20 a year in rent. When, through one of history's stranger quirks, Handel's former employer became England's George I, the expatriate composer was finally obliged to account for his absenteeism. A popular story has it that Handel, who would eventually become a naturalised Englishman in 1727, was happily reconciled with the newly royal George Louis at a Royal Party on the River Thames. In any event, he did win the support of the King to found the Royal Academy of Music as a venue for performances of opera, among them several of his own works. It was at 25 Brook Street that Handel wrote *Zadok The Priest*, *Israel In Egypt*, *Belshazzar* and – in a scarcely believable frenzy of creativity lasting just three weeks – *The Messiah*.

He put down roots here in Mayfair ... for which premises he paid £20 a year in rent

George Frederic Handel

- **THE WIGMORE HALL** (Tube: BOND STREET), built in 1901 at a cost of £100,000 by the German piano firm Bechstein, was intended to provide that company with an imposing but intimate venue for recitals next door to its Wigmore Street showrooms. Bechstein Hall, as it was originally called, opened in May of the year it was built to reveal **Thomas Collcutt**'s assured Renaissance-style interior design featuring alabaster and marble walls, flooring and stairway. Collcutt's other notable London buildings included the Imperial Institute (of which only the central tower remains today as part of Imperial College) and The Savoy Hotel (**see WC2**), which was more an implementation of **Richard D'Oyly Carte**'s own ideas and has been much altered over the years.

Bechstein Hall's first concert featured the virtuoso pianist **Ferruccio Busoni** and the building immediately won accolades for its impressive acoustics. The venue subsequently had no problem attracting major artists and over the years **Arthur Schnabel**, **Pablo de Sarasate**, **Artur Rubinstein**, **Percy Grainger**, **Myra Hess**, and **Charles-Camille Saint-Saëns** all performed there.

Audiences and performers have all been struck – not necessarily favourably – by the arts-and-crafts-style mural inside the cupola above the stage. It was designed by Frank Lynn Jenkins and fairly drips with meaning, apparently seeking to depict humanity's striving to capture the great abstraction of Music. This is the kind of emblematic painting that needs a user's manual if the viewer is to identify all the *dramatis personæ* that come together in an alle-

gorical traffic jam of ciphers and symbols. The central figure is apparently the Soul of Music who, gazing upwards, seems smitten by the sight of The Genius of Harmony who takes the form of a ball of fire. Beyond a tangled network of thorns Everyman is shown to be either ensnared by soulless materialism or seeking the inspiration of music. Supporting a musician in his labours is Love, depicted with roses in her hand, while on the opposite side of the tableau stands Psyche similarly acting as cheerleader to a composer who is transcribing music on a scroll. This picture was carefully restored as part of Wigmore Hall's recent refurbishment, for which those who like this kind of thing can be glad.

The original Hall had gone through a troubled period when, with the outbreak of World War I, its owners discovered that doing business as a German firm in London was not going to be easy. The Board of Trade finally wound up the declining Bechstein business and in 1916, sold the entire assets (including studios, offices, warehouses, 137 pianos, and the Hall itself) for just over half of what the Hall alone had cost to build. The lucky purchaser was the department store Debenham & Freebody who got it all for £56,500. Reopening as Wigmore Hall in 1917 the venue continued to attract world class artists and the roll call included **Elisabeth Schwarzkopf**, **Sergei Prokofiev**, **Paul Hindemith**, **Andres Segovia**, **Benjamin Britten**, **Francis Poulenc**, **Shura Cherkassky**, **The Amadeus Quartet**, and **Jacqueline du Pré**. The Wigmore Hall still presents some 400 concerts a year and has a reputation for giving artists their London débuts, as well as attracting established artists.

The Board of Trade finally wound up the declining Bechstein business and in 1916, sold the entire assets (including studios, offices, warehouses, 137 pianos, and the Hall itself)

Number **18 GREAT MARLBOROUGH STREET** (Tube: OXFORD CIRCUS) sports an inscription to mark a stay by **Ferenc** (a.k.a. Franz) **Liszt**. Once the inscription was bolder, but now it is in discreet gold leaf on light stone cladding, perhaps so as not to detract from the logo of the people who are currently paying the rent. This largely overlooked location is just one of many

London sites at which Liszt, always on the move, stayed on his prodigious travels. His other London visits saw him as a house and dinner guest all over the capital. By the time he was reaching the end of his life he seemed to have forged an unlikely bond with the south London suburb of Penge, where the music publisher **Henry Littleton** lived. In 1886, after emerging from religious semi-seclusion, Liszt came back to London for a final triumphant visit. When a party of friends and admirers sailed to Calais to accompany him back to Littleton's house, the chairman of the London, Chatham and Dover Railway agreed to let the boat train make an unscheduled stop at Penge railway station. There the disembarking composer was greeted with a speech in Hungarian, a bouquet and a rousing welcome by a crowd of a hundred. The visit continued with a round of social engagements in London and a trip to Windsor Castle to play for **Queen Victoria**.

This largely overlooked location is just one of many London sites at which Liszt, always on the move, stayed on his prodigious travels

Before moving with his father, mother and sister to Ebury Street near Victoria (**see SW1**), **Wolfgang Amadeus Mozart** lived at a house on the site of the current number **20 FRITH STREET** (Tube: TOTTENHAM COURT ROAD or LEICESTER SQUARE). This was in 1764 and 1765, the premises belonging to one Thomas Williamson, a corset-maker with whom they lodged. To call the young Mozart a prodigy was perhaps to understate the case, as the following advertisement taken from The Public Advertiser of March 11th 1765 suggests. "For the Benefit of Master MOZART, of eight years, and Miss MOZART, of twelve years of age, prodigies by Nature, before their Departure from England, which will be in six Weeks Time. THERE will be performed at the End of this Month, or the Beginning of April next, a Concert of Vocal and Instrumental MUSIC. Tickets at Half a Guinea Each. To be had of Mr. Mozart, at Mr Williamson's in Thrift-street (Frith Street's original name), Soho; where those Ladies and Gentlemen, who will honour him with their Company from Twelve to Three in the Afternoon, any Day in the Week except Tuesday and Friday, may, by each taking a Ticket, gratify their Curiosity and not only hear this young Music master and his Sister perform in private; but likewise try his surprising musical capacity, by giving him anything to play at Sight, or any Music without Bass which he will write upon the Spot, without recurring to his Harpsichord". Ah, but could the lad juggle, walk a tightrope or ride a unicycle?

To call the young Mozart a prodigy was perhaps to understate the case

Wolfgang Amadeus Mozart

- Number **2 MANCHESTER SQUARE** (Tube: BOND STREET) was the residence of the conductor and composer **Sir Julius Benedict**. A blue plaque marks the house where he lived from 1845 until his death in 1885. Manchester Square is a pleasant Marylebone square that also includes Hertford House, home of The Wallace Collection, and once accommodated an EMI office building (number 20, now demolished and replaced) in

which **The Beatles** were famously photographed for the sleeve of their first British album. Benedict was a German by birth, the son of a Jewish banker, who became a respected conductor of operas and oratorios and a familiar figure at both Her Majesty's Theatre and Drury Lane. A pupil of **Carl Maria von Weber**, he became musical director to **Jenny Lind** (Johanna Maria Lind), the Swedish-born operatic and oratorio soprano who had a long association with London. Over the years, Benedict was visited at his Manchester Square home by **Giacomo Meyerbeer**, **Louis-Hector Berlioz**, **Charles Gounod** and **Charles-Camille Saint-Saëns** among other musical luminaries. As a composer Benedict is today largely forgotten. During his lifetime he was well known for his opera *The Lily of Killarney* (1863) and the oratorio *St Peter* (1870). A favourite of royalty, he was knighted by **Queen Victoria** and received an array of decorations from various European sovereigns.

Over the years, Benedict was visited at his Manchester Square home by Giacomo Meyerbeer, Louis-Hector Berlioz, Charles Gounod and Charles-Camille Saint-Saëns

Number **48 DOVER STREET** (Tube: GREEN PARK) was home to **Frédéric Chopin** throughout the summer of 1848. On this trip he went to the opera to hear **Jenny Lind (see The Royal Opera House, WC2)** where the presence of **Queen Victoria** in the audience impressed him less than that of the **Duke of Wellington** "sitting beneath the royal box like an old monarchical watch-dog in his kennel, beneath his mistress". Chopin also attended a performance of The Philharmonic Society, which English venture he dismissed as being "like their roast beef or turtle soup...strong and efficient but nothing more". For a payment of 20 guineas Chopin himself played at Duchess of Sutherland's home in the presence of Queen Victoria, Prince Albert and "watch-dog" Wellington. Money seemed to be something of a problem for Chopin who, on being advised that his 20-guinea fee was rather high, concluded sniffily that "money is tight here". Taking on pupils he soon found that at least one was a bad credit risk having "already left for the country, leaving nine lessons unpaid". Like many other foreign visitors Chopin was ever ready to launch into a diatribe against the climate and its effects upon Londoners. "If only London were not so black, and the people not so heavy and dull and if only there were no fogs or smells of soot" he wrote home – not entirely logically – "I might have learned English by now". Francophile Chopin simply did not find the English *simpatico*. "They consider everything in terms of money; they like art only because it's a *luxury*".

A performance of The Philharmonic Society…he dismissed as being "like their roast beef or turtle soup… strong and efficient but nothing more"

- Number **6 YORK STREET** (Tube:
- BAKER STREET) was for over forty
- years home to **Francesco Berger**,
- composer, pianist and Secretary to
- the Philharmonic Society.
- In his administrative role
- he commissioned **Saint-**
- **Saëns**' *Third Symphony*
- and Dvořák's *Seventh Sym-*
- *phony*. It was at his
- Marylebone address that
- Berger entertained **Pyotr**
- **Tchaikovsky** in March of
- 1888. Dining in with the
- great Russian composer
- provided Berger with anec-
- dotes on which to dine out
- for several of the many
- years left to him (he died
- just short of his 100th
- birthday). "Like most for-
- eigners, Tchaikovsky was
- fond of English food,
- cooked English fashion,"
- noted Berger wrongly (for

a more representative European opinion **see Wagner**'s views on English cuisine in **Balcombe Street, NW1**.) Note too that Tchaikovsky, in his role as a clerk in St Petersburg, was once seen absentmindedly tearing pieces from an official doc- ument and munching at them steadily until he realised too late that he had consumed the whole thing.). "His conversation carried on in French and German…was easy without being brilliant," continued Berger, "and in all he said there was apparent the modest, gentle spirit which was so characteristic of the man". Berger did not fail to notice, however, that his guest never spoke of politics. "If in the course of con- versation that topic cropped up, (Tchaikovsky) would remark that music and art generally were fit matters for musicians to discuss – not politics."

Tchaikovsky, in his role as a clerk in St Petersburg, was once seen absentmindedly tearing pieces from an official document and munching at them steadily

GREAT PORTLAND STREET (Tube: GREAT PORTLAND STREET) has seen its share of musical visitors. At number 103 stood a building where Jakob Ludwig Felix Mendelssohn-Bartholdy a.k.a **Felix Mendelssohn** lodged intermittently during 1829, 1832 and 1833. (The current building is invisible beneath construction sheeting at the time of writing). Mendelssohn's landlord, a German named Heinke, was an ironmonger and locksmith who once had the doubtful pleasure of opening a locked door at nearby number 91 Great Portland Street in 1826. Behind it was the corpse of **Carl Maria von Weber** who had heroically but unwisely risked London's sulphurous fogs to earn money for his family by completing and conducting his opera *Oberon* here. When Herr Heinke gained access to the second floor bedroom he found the late maestro surrounded by his clothing arranged in neat piles ready to be packed for the trip back home he was never going to make in this life. Six years later Mendelssohn was ensconced at number 103 when **Thomas Attwood** conducted the world première of Fingal's Cave at The King's Theatre. Life with the Heinkes agreed with Mendelssohn, and the dishes he was served there – particularly mutton chops and bread-and-butter pudding – he liked so much as to request as a nightcap following a concert. Mendelssohn wrote of London "That smoky nest is fated to be forever my favourite city; my heart swells when I think of it". Today's enlightened dietary wisdom combined with Mendelssohn's death at the age of 38 prompts the sad reflection that perhaps it was not pride that enlarged his heart, but Mrs Heinke's cooking.

Mendelssohn's landlord…once had the doubtful pleasure of opening a locked door at nearby number 91 Great Portland Street in 1826. Behind it was the corpse of Carl Maria von Weber

In 1820 the German violinist, composer and conductor **Louis** (**Ludwig**) **Spohr** made the first of his six tours of England. He stayed at **1a DEVONSHIRE STREET** (Tube: BAKER STREET) and he was at this time considered to be a great composer, spoken of in the same breath as **Bach** and **Beethoven**. He had taught himself composition by studying the scores of **Wolfgang Amadeus Mozart** and studied violin with the leader of the orchestra in his hometown of Brunswick. He even toured Italy with the violin virtuoso **Niccolò Paganini** at one point. Upon arrival in London he immediately committed a major social gaffe. On his first morning he was to meet with the directors of The Philharmonic Society and, wishing to make a good impression – or at least an impression – he put on "a bright red Turkish shawl-pattern waistcoat". Whether this was advisable or not *per se*, is open to question but since George III had just died it was perhaps not the wisest choice. However, secure in the knowledge that the waistcoat was "considered on the Continent to be a most elegant article" the heavily-built Spohr set off only to attract the immediate derision of passers-by. In the end he was pursued by a number of people mouthing abuse which, having little English, he failed to understand, at least in the specifics. On arrival, matters were explained to him and he swiftly returned to Devonshire Street to change his waistcoat for a more sombre one. Spohr, in fact, seemed to have little luck with crowds. Minus the Turkish waistcoat he was adored in London and was constantly besieged by autograph hunters. Leaving the capital by steamer in 1843 he said dryly that there could now no longer be a music lover in England who did not have

Leaving the capital by steamer in 1843 he said dryly that there could now no longer be a music lover in England who did not have his autograph. Right on cue a rowing boat full of autograph hunters appeared alongside

his autograph. Right on cue a rowing boat full of autograph hunters appeared alongside and kept pace with the steamer until Gravesend was sighted and Spohr had finished signing. Today it is difficult to believe that in the early 1800s the overture to Spohr's Jessonda was performed 24 times at Philharmonic Socciety concerts, while during the same period the overture to Mozart's *The Marriage of Figaro* was played on just 10 occasions. Back home Spohr became court conductor at Kassel in 1821 although in his later years his political radicalism earned him the displeasure of his patron, the elector of Hesse-Kassel, who pensioned him off in 1857. Shortly afterwards, he broke his left arm and was no longer able to play the violin.

The Sicilian operatic composer **Vincenzo Bellini** lived at **3 OLD BURLINGTON STREET** (Tube: PICCADILLY CIRCUS) from April to August 1833. Born into a family of musicians, Bellini had produced his first works while still a student at the Naples Conservatory; later he gained the patronage of an important impresario who commissioned Bianca e Fernando for the Naples opera. Its success led to other commissions: *Il Pirata*, written for Milan's La Scala, won Bellini an international reputation. With Italian librettist **Felice Romani** he collaborated for his next six operas, the best known of which were *I Capuleti ed i Montecchi*, (based on Romeo and Juliet); *La Sonnambula*; and *Norma*. At the beginning of his London visit Bellini attended a performance of *La Cenerèntola* at The King's Theatre whose audience also included **Felix Mendelssohn** and **Niccolò Paganini**. Bellini and Paganini were also both present at the world première of Mendelssohn's *Italian Symphony* conducted by the composer at the Hanover Square Rooms on May 13th. During Bellini's stay at Old Burlington Street several of his works were staged: *La Sonnambula* at Drury Lane; and *Il Pirata*, *I Capuleti ed i Montecchi* and *Norma* at The King's Theatre. Fêted, Bellini confessed to finding himself "in the midst of a world of beautiful women, truly, of celestial beauties" although he was quick to point out that "I indulge in nothing but sentiment". His reasons for foregoing temptation he identified as being both the brevity of his stay and putting "more value upon friendship than upon love, so as not to run the risk of acquiring a wife".

Bellini confessed to finding himself "in the midst of a world of beautiful women, `truly, of celestial beauties"

Number **18 GREAT PULTENEY STREET** (Tube: PICCADILLY CIRCUS) was the London home of the violinist, conductor, impresario and composer **Johann Peter Salomon** who successfully coaxed **Joseph Haydn** to come to London with promise of commissions and performances. Haydn arrived on New Year's Day, 1791, perhaps not sorry to get away from the disdainful wife who used his manuscripts as pastry pan liners. The following 18 months lived up to all expectations. There were meetings with eminent musicians and the praise bestowed on Haydn had a great impact on his creative work. During his stay he had ample opportunity to write half a dozen or so major pieces in between writing about the weather. "The fog was so thick you could have spread it on bread," Haydn noted, bringing new and vivid imagery to a familiar complaint. "I had to light the lights at 11 a.m. so I could write," he added, less originally. Salomon had commissioned six symphonies and twenty shorter pieces from Haydn, the symphonies now collectively being known as *The London Symphonies* (or occasionally The Salomon Symphonies). During his stay Haydn directed the world premieres of symphonies 93, 94, 95, 96, 97 and 98 at the Hanover Square Rooms. All of these works were written in London and performed directly from manuscript. A relatively cool reception back in Austria prompted him to make a second trip to London in 1794 where he was again greeted warmly although this time more as an old friend than a fêted new talent.

Haydn arrived on New Year's Day, 1791, perhaps not sorry to get away from the disdainful wife who used his manuscripts as pastry pan liners

Foreign musicians visited London for many reasons, but rarely, it seems, for their health and not very often for the food. **Gioachino Rossini** was perhaps unique in coming exclusively for financial profit... and succeeding wildly. He stayed at **90 REGENT STREET** (Tube: PICCADILLY CIRCUS) from December 13th 1823 until July 26th 1824 and his sojourn began on the now depressingly familiar note of illness – did any 18th or 19th century visiting musician not suffer a collapse of health upon setting foot in London? With Rossini it was the boat trip that laid him up and he was obliged to spend a week at his Regent Street address before he even felt well enough to get out of bed. But as soon as he did, the cash register started ringing. His plan was to accompany his wife, the diva **Isabella Colbran**, at private engagements, to give a few lessons and to conduct eight of his operas. He accomplished all of these things and met King George IV. "I received attentions that would be difficult to parallel anywhere else," Rossini noted afterwards. The only composition to come out of the London visit was the cantata Il Pianto delle Muse in Morte di Lord Byron, a tribute to the poet who, since April 24th 1824, was not only mad, bad and dangerous to know but dead as well. The cantata was performed in London on July 9th, less than three weeks before Rossini was to leave. When he did his pockets were sagging with 175,000 francs, a sum that supported him for the remaining 44 years of his life. "I never made enough from my art to be able to save anything – except for my stay in England," Rossini later said. "And in London I earned money not as a composer but as an accompanist." Rossini had charged the relatively high fee of £50

"I never made enough from my art to be able to save anything – except for my stay in England," Rossini later said

"… in London, musicians will do anything and everything to make money. I saw the oddest things…"

when he and his wife participated in musical soirées. "We took part in about 60 of them," he said, "and that, after all, was worth the bother. By the way, in London, musicians will do anything and everything to make money. I saw the oddest things there…" Sadly Rossini did not elaborate. What had he seen? **Felix Mendelssohn** playing the piano in the local pub? **Hector Berlioz** doing card tricks on the pavement? We may never know. Following the profitable London trip, the couple went back to Paris, which was then the centre of the cultural world, and where "Monsieur Crescendo" as he was not unaffectionately known, was fêted all over again.

- **HANOVER SQUARE ROOMS**, Hanover Square (Tube: OXFORD CIRCUS). All that is left of the legendary Hanover Square Rooms is the square in which they were located. They once stood on the east side on a site now occupied by unremarkable business premises that include a JAL airlines office. The venue thrived from 1775 to 1874 as one of London's major concert halls for most its life;

and was finally demolished in 1900. The Hanover Square Rooms concerts were begun by the creative partnership of pianist and composer **Johann Christian Bach** and *viola da gamba* player **Karl Friedrich Abel**. Johann was the eleventh son of **Johann Sebastian Bach** and was known as "the London Bach" because he spent much of the last 25 years of his life in the city. Abel was the last of the great players of the now revived but once forgotten *viola da gamba* or viol (an instrument with a gut-fretted neck and tuned like a Renaissance lute). The roll call of famous players and composers who subsequently appeared at the Hanover Square Rooms is impressive: **Clara Schumann**, **Niccolò Paganini**, **Anton Rubinstein**, **Joseph Joachim**, **Richard Wagner** and **Ferenc Liszt** were among them. Following the destruction of The Argyll rooms by fire, The Philharmonic Concerts were relocated here from 1833.

Johann was the eleventh son of Johann Sebastian Bach and was known as "the London Bach" because he spent much of the last 25 years of his life in the city

ST PATRICK'S ROMAN CATHOLIC CHURCH stands on the corner of Soho Square and Sutton Row (Tube: TOTTENHAM COURT ROAD), and is one of two churches in this small square. St Patrick's brings a devout touch to what was previously a boldly secular site. Here in the 1760s and 1770s **Theresa Cornelys** ran a "Temple of Festivity" in what was then known as Carlisle House. Cornelys was an opera singer and a businesswoman with what might be described as a colourful past. Although those worthies **Johann Christian Bach** and **Karl Friedrich Abel** were known to take part in *bona fide* concerts at Carlisle House, not all of Mrs Cornelys' visitors were looking for the sort of good time provided by pianoforte and viol. Thus she was arraigned for keeping a "common disorderly house" in 1771. A more sheltered woman might have found this insupportable, but Cornelys had been around the block a few times. At the age of 17 she had moved in with a 76 year-old Venetian senator, and a little later she bore a son to **Giovanni Giacomo Casanova**. Her marriage to dancer **Angelo Pompeati** did not survive his successful attempt to disembowel himself, and so his widow began a faltering operatic career in London, Hamburg and Copenhagen. After a couple of brief liaisons with minor members of European royalty, the resilient Cornelys opened a Knightsbridge breakfast bar whose menu, perhaps unwisely, featured asses' milk. Incredibly it was this venture that finished her off. She went bankrupt and ended her days in London's Fleet Prison.

At the age of 17 she had moved in with a 76 year-old Venetian senator, and a little later she bore a son to Casanova

- **BROADCASTING HOUSE**, Portland Place (Tube: OXFORD CIRCUS) is the headquarters of the British Broadcasting Corporation (BBC), a publicly financed broadcasting organisation originally run along dour paternalistic lines that are inevitably dubbed Reithian after **John Reith**, the BBC's general manager from 1922 and director general from 1927 to 1938. These were very innocent times by today's standards. On Good Friday 1930 radio listeners to the evening news were told simply, 'There is no news.' Piano music was broadcast instead. **Gustav Holst** was the first composer commissioned by the BBC. Holst's *The Morning of the Year* was completed in 1927. **Sir Edward Elgar** was similarly commissioned to write his Third Symphony but it remained uncompleted on his death. The BBC took over the Promenade Concerts in 1927, just one step in democratising

the availability of classical music nationally and – through its World Service – globally. Conservative rather than responsive in the early years, the BBC was often out of touch with public taste. During World War II portentous music was broadcast, supposedly to match the *Zeitgeist* but all it did was depress. "I'd rather face German guns than hear any more organ music…" complained one listener. When **Vera Lynn** broadcast more accessible patriotic music the BBC Governors' response was "Popularity noted, but deplored". **Sir Adrian Boult** was made Musical Director of the BBC in 1930 and its Conductor In Chief in 1941. BBC outside broadcasts made minority concerts available to everyone. Today, in a much-changed world of broadcasting, the BBC still transmits many hundreds of hours of classical music every year.

On Good Friday 1930 radio listeners to the evening news were told simply, 'There is no news.'

BBC building detail

The Czech composer...seems to have been one of those gifted men who somehow do not travel well

Number **12 HINDE STREET** (Tube: BOND STREET) was the London home of the German pianist and composer **Oscar Beringer** during the 1880s and 1890s. He had been a pupil of **Ignaz Moscheles** and **Karl Tausig** and he was the soloist for the first London performance of **Brahms'** *Second Piano Concerto* in 1882. He also gave the British première of **Antonin Dvořák's** *Piano Concerto* at the Crystal Palace in 1883. The following year Dvořák came to stay with him at Hinde Street for most of the month of March. It was one of nine trips to the capital made by the Czech composer who, on the evidence, seems to have been one of those gifted men who somehow do not travel well, with a capacity for making social gaffes when abroad (**see The Langham**, also **W1**). During this particular visit he was given to rising at dawn and taking a stroll. He seemed to take quite a long one on the day he came upon the exclusive Athenæum Club in Pall Mall and, blithely identifying it as a café, went in, sat down and ordered a cup of coffee. He was ejected shortly afterwards. He still returned to London in 1895 and 1896 to conduct premières of two more works.

- **Eduard Hanslick**, the Prague-born music critic and author of books on music and concert life stayed at **17 (LOWER) SEYMOUR STREET** (Tube: MARBLE ARCH) on the second of his two trips to London in 1886. (The street is now just Seymour Street). Parodied as Beckmesser in Die Meistersinger by the racially ungenerous **Wagner**, Hanslick had been music critic for the Wiener Zeitung and later became music editor of both Die Presse and Neue Freie Presse in Vienna. An excellent pianist himself, he was an influential arbiter of taste and the possessor of an elegant if combative literary style. A conservative, he rejected Wagner and **Liszt** while supporting the music of **Schumann** and **Brahms**. The next summer he

published his findings in Neue Freie Presse, including a damning review of what he saw as **Sir Arthur Sullivan**'s uninspired conducting of Mozart's *Symphony No. 40* ("never lifted his eyes from the score, as if he were reading it for the first time") and the performance's overall impact ("plodded along, for better or worse, badly played without feeling or elegance"). Sullivan, whom he had met on his first visit, was obviously not a favourite with Hanslick who also went to see *The Mikado*. "Sir Arthur Sullivan's music is not notable for its originality or any traces of genius," he wrote, going on to damn with faint praise by allowing that Sullivan, although working in a secondary genre, had at least managed to be "melodious and amusing for an entire evening".

In London to assess the city's musical life, he came and he observed and he did not much like what he saw

Britton died at the age of 60, "after being terrified by a ventriloquist"

JERUSALEM PASSAGE and **AYLESBURY STREET** (Tube: FARRINGDON) form a corner where the depot of singing coal merchant **Thomas Britton** ("the musical small-coal man") was located. Britton (1654-1714) merited a mention in Jonathan Swift's A Description of the Morning: "The Smallcoal-Man was heard with Cadence deep/'Till drown'd in Shriller Notes of Chimney-Sweep". Britton became famous as a pioneer of the public concert. If not the first to do it (**John Banester** had tried a few years earlier), Britton was certainly the most celebrated. Performances took place in a room above his coal depot to which access was gained by a steep, narrow external staircase that tested the resolve and the agility of some members of the audience, especially women in wide and complicated robes. Once reached, the concert room was hardly spacious. It was described by one Ned Ward, a neighbouring publican with aspirations to being a social commentator. He wrote: "His House is not much higher than a Canary Pipe, and the Window of his State-Room, but very little bigger than the Bunghole of a Cask". Despite this, Britton's concerts attracted universal praise for the quality of the music. The most famous performer was **George Frederic Handel** who played a five-stop organ above the coal depot on one occasion. Apparently a man without enemies, Thomas Britton was liked by all, a fact which somehow makes the nature of his death seem even more bizarre than it already was. In circumstances about which history is maddeningly vague, Britton died at the age of 60, "after being terrified by a ventriloquist".

- **SADLER'S WELLS THEATRE**, Rosebery Avenue (Tube: ANGEL) has been a place of entertainment for over 300 years, ever since one **Dick Sadler** opened his 'musick house' in the 1680s. The happy accident of finding an ancient well in the grounds suggested to the enterprising owner a profitable marketing angle, and thus Sadler's Wells Spa/Music Hall entertainment complex was born. The emphasis moved back to entertainment at the beginning of the 18th century and over the years the building would be reconstructed four times before the present day Lottery-funded improvements began in the late 1990s. The comic actor **Joseph Grimaldi** (who to his eternal discredit helped to establish Britain's direst form of public entertainment, the pantomime) was Sadler's Wells' star performer in the early 19th century when the other staples were light opera and variety acts. Under visionary actor/manager **Samuel Phelps**, Sadler's Wells turned to legitimate theatre in the mid-19th century but after his departure in 1862 the place went into decline, eventually taking turns as a roller-skating rink and a boxing arena. Re-opening as a theatre in 1879, it became a music hall and then just before the dawn of the 20th century turned into a cinema. No doubt exhausted, it closed in 1915. In 1925 the formidable **Lilian Baylis** decided to make it a northern outpost for her work at The Old Vic in south London, where she might concentrate on opera and ballet. She engaged **Ninette de Valois** to develop classical ballet and between them they created and nurtured, at Dick Sadler's old place, The Royal Ballet and the English National Opera (**see The Coliseum WC2**).

Finding an ancient well in the grounds suggested to the enterprising owner a profitable marketing angle

This chapel only took on its present name in the 1950s, being previously known as St Cecilia's Chapel in honour of the patron saint of musicians

ST SEPULCHRE'S, Holborn Viaduct, (Tube: ST PAUL'S) is a rather unimpressive church from the outside but one with a splendid interior. It has unusually rich musical associations that include its Musicians' Chapel. The church, originally dedicated to St Edmund, was founded in 1137 but its location just outside the northwest city gate made it a logical starting point for The Crusaders; in this context an association with The Church of the Holy Sepulchre in Jerusalem led to its rededication in the 15th century. The Great Fire of London spared little of the original building although still visible is a scorched stone basin set into the west wall. All that is left of an organ built by **Renatus Harris** in 1677 is the casing, but **George Frederic Handel** and **Felix Mendelssohn** both played that original organ and it survived long enough for the youthful **Henry Wood** (see **4 Elsworthy Road NW3**) to take lessons on it. Wood's ashes now reside in the Musicians' Chapel which also vividly commemorates **John Ireland** and **Dame Nellie Melba**. This chapel only took on its present name in the 1950s, being previously known as St Cecilia's Chapel in honour of the patron saint of musicians. Cecilia was a Roman aristocrat so affected by the music at her wedding ceremony that she abruptly called off the nuptials and dedicated her virginity to God. Later she was martyred for her faith. This seems a somehow unsatisfactory story but perhaps one that might lend itself to a light comedy movie... No Wedding and a Martyrdom, perhaps?

- **THE BARBICAN** (Tube: BARBICAN) is a large mixed-use complex in The City of London (the capital's business district). Its architecture is ugly beyond belief, but it bristles with cultural activities and is especially strong in music events. The area was covered with a warren of small streets and warehouses until it was bombed in World War II. Post-war renovation plans came late but, like the road to Hell, they were paved with good intentions. The Barbican plan was launched by a proposal from Britain's then Minister of Housing, Duncan Sandys. In 1956 (interestingly, the year before he appeared in sexually explicit Polaroid photographs with Douglas Fairbanks Junior and Margaret, Duchess of Argyll) Duncan Sandys virtuously

advanced the idea that the area should become "a genuine residential neighbourhood incorporating schools, shops, open spaces and other amenities… even if this means foregoing a more remunerative return on the land." The City of London, bustling by day but dead at night, accepted the plan in an attempt to reverse a severe population decline in its famous square mile (down from 125,000 to some 5,000 in a century). Building work began in the late Sixties, and the Barbican Centre itself was started in October 1971. The design was by Chamberlin, Powell & Bon, a practice much influenced by **Le Corbusier**'s whimsical notions about social housing. The original plan had included finding a site for **The Guildhall School of Music and Drama** (then in Blackfriars) and to this it was decided to add a London base for the **Royal**

The complex was generally so badly designed that it was impossible to navigate on foot without getting lost

Shakespeare Company and a home for **The London Symphony Orchestra**. The strike-ridden Barbican project would take a staggering 27 years to complete, and when it was finally finished it was not just the shock of the new that earned it criticism: this intimidating example of Brutalism was constructed out of easy-stain concrete, with windswept walkways and hostile stairwells. The complex was generally so badly designed that it was impossible to navigate on foot without getting lost. Eventually the operators were obliged to paint different coloured lines on the ground throughout to aid navigation. So why venture into The Barbican? Well, its music programmes are varied and numerous and its concert hall, home to The London Symphony Orchestra, is a good one. The Guildhall School of Music and Drama was finally accommodated in 1977 and now enjoys a reputation for teaching a very broad musical curriculum; **Sir Joseph Barnby** was one of the School's principals. The Barbican Library also contains a good **Music Library** and a valuable **Music Performance Research Centre** where many rare recordings may be listened to on the premises. Perhaps most surprising of all, the complex can, in the summer, seem to be something of what it originally aspired to be: a pleasant meeting place where outside musical performances and other events take place surrounded by open spaces in the form of a lake, lawns, planted areas, landscaped terraces and well-maintained gardens. The social housing has become almost exclusively a privately-owned estate, but in warm weather the public spaces can be recommended to anyone with a sure sense of direction and a tolerance of discoloured concrete.

Perhaps most surprising of all, the complex can, in the summer, seem to be something of what it originally aspired to be

- **Anton Bruckner**, the Austrian composer, made only one trip to Britain. It was during the summer of 1871 and for its duration he stayed at Seyd's German Guesthouse which was located at **39 FINSBURY SQUARE** (Tube: M O O R G A T E). Bruckner, who wrote several highly original and monumental symphonies, was also an organist and teacher who composed sacred

and secular choral music. The occasion of his visit was a series of celebratory recitals at The Royal Albert Hall (**see SW7**) given by international performers to inaugurate the new organ. Bruckner was representing Austria; **Charles-Camille Saint-Saëns** represented France. Bruckner gave six recitals that were so well received he was invited to give four additional performances at The Crystal Palace (by this time removed from its original location in Hyde Park and rebuilt at Sydenham Hill in South London). There he played to a euphoric audience of 70,000 whose reception moved him to write to a friend: "Tremendous applause, always unending. Requests for encores …heaps of compliments. Everywhere my name appears in letters bigger than myself!" Elated by his success, Bruckner began writing his second symphony while still a guest at Finsbury Square.

"Everywhere my name appears in letters bigger than myself!"

Anton Bruckner

Alpha Place, NW1, was demolished to make way for **MARYLEBONE STATION** (Tube: MARYLEBONE). However, it was still there in the summer of 1862 when **Giuseppe Verdi** stayed at number 43. Verdi had first visited the city in 1847, and on that occasion he had the same horrified response that everyone from **Wagner** to **Chopin** seemed to experience on arriving in The Smoke. "I found the London climate horrifying," Verdi wrote unpromisingly, although he did go on to say that otherwise he was "extremely delighted with the city". This trip had been undertaken to complete and conduct *I Masnadieri* which had been commissioned by Her Majesty's Theatre (**see SW1**) and Verdi professed himself quite impressed with "the beauty of the streets, the cleanliness of the houses". He made three more business trips to London before the 1862 visit which was undertaken for the world première of *Inno delle Nazione*, written for the International Exhibition of that year. Something of a star, Verdi was by now the target of a particularly English type of autograph hunter whose habit of sending the maestro a self-addressed envelope for the purpose of signing and mailing back an autograph struck Verdi as odd. "In other countries people who want autographs...get themselves introduced," he grumbled. "Over here I get letters through the post. Who the hell they are, I've not the slightest idea." Verdi returned again in 1874 for the **Handel** Festival at The Crystal Palace and his final trip was in 1875 when he conducted the British première of his Requiem at The Royal Albert Hall (**see SW7**).

Verdi professed himself quite impressed with "the beauty of the streets, the cleanliness of the houses"

- At the end of the 19th century the present **BALCOMBE STREET** (Tube: MARYLEBONE) was known as Milton Street. At number 31 (today number 65), **Richard Wagner** stayed at the home of one **Ferdinand Praeger** in March 1855 before moving closer to Regent's Park. The park was to become a favourite haunt throughout Wagner's four-month stay in the capital during which time he conducted eight Philharmonic concerts. The premises to which he moved, 22 Portland Terrace,

have now disappeared completely along with the entire street (it was near the North Gate of Regent's Park). This Wagnerian stay in northwest London was punctuated by frequent visits to the royal park where the architect of the 17-hour *Der Ring des Nibelungen* apparently enjoyed the simple pleasures watching sheep graze and feeding the ducks. He also took the opportunity to attend a number of oratorio performances that he judged to be more suited to the English Protestant temperament than opera. "An evening spent in listening to an oratorio may be regarded as a sort of service," Wagner observed, not entirely approvingly. "Everybody holds a Handel piano score the way that one holds a prayer book in church." However London's most potent impact upon him, as on most other 19th century foreign visitors, was the hostile climate and its effects. On this subject Wagner later managed to

"Everybody holds a Handel piano score the way that one holds a prayer book in church."

Sixteen years earlier he had stayed at an inn in Old Compton Street where he was constantly enraged by the sound of the organ grinders outside

summon a suitably dramatic response to the *Sturm und Regen* that for him linked this particular London visit with "the all-absorbing memory of almost uninterrupted ill-health, caused, primarily no doubt, by the state of the London climate at that season of the year, which is notorious throughout the world." Since he was in London for spring and summer, one wonders how he would have reacted to a winter visit. "I had a perpetual cold, and I therefore followed the advice of my friends to take a heavy English diet by way of resisting the effects of the air, but this did not improve matters in the slightest." Understandably his attempts to orchestrate *Die Walküre* suffered from this twin assault of bad weather and a leaden diet, and he managed to complete only a few hundred pages before giving up and turning instead to diversionary reading matter that matched the mood. "In absolute despair I plunged into Dante," he wrote afterwards. "The Inferno, indeed, became a never-to-be-forgotten reality in the London atmosphere." All in all Wagner did not seem to have much luck in London. Sixteen years earlier he had stayed at an inn in Old Compton Street where he was constantly enraged by the sound of the organ grinders outside, admittedly a sound not conducive to the creation of grandiose operas. Twenty years later he visited a well-known Harley Street ophthalmologist where he ordered some spectacles to be sent on to him in Germany. Back in the fatherland, recovering from the debilitating effects of his latest trip to London, he eventually received the spectacles only to break them the same day.

Opening its doors for the first time in 1823 **THE ROYAL ACADEMY OF MUSIC**, Marylebone Road (Tube: BAKER STREET) is England's oldest musical training institution, although it has only occupied these premises since 1912. Prior to that the Academy, based upon an institution founded by **George Frederic Handel (see 25 Brook Street, W1)** had been located in Tenterden Street, off Hanover Square. It was there that its first principal, **William Crotch**, presided over an intake of residential pupils of primary school age. Precocious talent was much admired at the time, but if **Mozart** had been a prodigy at the age of eight **(see 20 Frith Street, W1)** Crotch made him look like a late developer. Ambidextrous and capable, when composing, of writing two staves simultaneously, Crotch was playing 'God Save The King' at the age of two and a half and supplying the bass part into the bargain. At the age of four, now a seasoned performer, he was giving public recitals in London. As a composer Crotch did not match his early promise and it is in the role of teacher and populariser of **Bach** that he is chiefly remembered. **William Sterndale Bennett** was both pupil and Principal of The Royal Academy of Music. **Sir Henry Wood** was a pupil here from 1886 and Reginald Kenneth Dwight, later to become **Sir Elton John**, won a scholarship to the Academy in 1958. From its original approach (uniformed children living in basic conditions with pianos in bedrooms and dining rooms) the Academy took on its more familiar modern curriculum with the move to these premises.

Precocious talent was much admired at the time, but if Mozart had been a prodigy at the age of eight ... Crotch made him look like a late developer

HANOVER TERRACE is a well-hidden little street close to the Hanover Gate entrance to Regent's Park (Tube: BAKER STREET). Today it lies in the shadow of the London Central Mosque, perhaps some sort of gentle irony since Hanover Terrace's point of interest is that number 10 was once the home of that most nationalistic of English composers **Ralph Vaughan Williams**. He studied at Trinity College, Cambridge and at the Royal College of Music under both **Sir Charles Villiers Stanford** and **Sir Charles Hubert Parry** (**see W8** for their houses and **SW7** for **The Royal College of Music**). A collector of folk music and a man much influenced by the English Tudor composers, Vaughan Williams was a composer who found his own voice and in doing so created a new musical language rooted in his own country. He lived at number 10 for five years until his death in 1958. While here he wrote *The England of Elizabeth*, *A Vision of Aeroplanes*, *Ten Blake Songs* and *Three Vocalises*. Visitors to the address included **Percy Grainger**, **Arthur Bliss**, **Adrian Boult**, **John Barbirolli**, **Grace Williams** and **Arthur Benjamin**. Vaughan Williams was also a friend of **Cecil Sharp**, the musician and indefatigable collector of English folk and dance melodies to which Vaughan Williams was so indebted. Cecil Sharp House, established in 1930 as a centre for the preservation of this work, is at 2 Regent's Park Road not too far away although its nearest tube is Camden Town. It houses the Vaughan Williams Memorial Library and, despite some financial difficulties in recent years, the centre is still in existence.

Vaughan Williams was a composer who found his own voice and in doing so created a new musical language rooted in his own country

- Number **4 ELSWORTHY ROAD**, just northwest of Primrose Hill (Tube: SWISS COTTAGE or ST JOHN'S WOOD) is one of those unremarkable looking premises that played host to a number of quite remarkable visitors over the years. The years in question were 1902 to 1937 during which time **Sir Henry Wood** lived here. Henry Joseph Wood was a key figure in the popularisation of orchestral music in England in the 20th century. Originally an organist, he studied composition at the Royal Academy of Music (**see SW7**) from 1886. In 1889 he toured as a conductor with the Arthur Rousbey Opera Company and later appeared with other opera companies. After helping to organise a series of **Wagner** concerts at the Queen's Hall, in 1895, he established there a season of Promenade Concerts that were to exert an immeasurable influence on English musical life. Starting with a popular repertory, Wood systematically broadened the appeal of his concerts. Wood's Promenade Concerts were managed from 1927 by the British Broadcasting Corporation (BBC) and after the destruction of the Queen's Hall in World War II they were transferred to their present home, the Royal Albert Hall (**see SW7**). In 1898 Wood had married the Russian singer **Olga Urusova**, who had formerly been his pupil. When she died he married **Muriel Greatorex** in 1911, the same year as he was knighted. Prior to the arrival of the new Lady Wood, number 4 Elsworthy Road saw several boisterous visitors: in 1902 **Charles-Camille Saint-Saëns** called and, upon being apologetically told by the first Mrs Wood that the curtains were at the cleaners, he rushed to the piano and, according to Wood, "pro-

"Saint–Saëns proceeded to improvise a free fantasia to express the horror of his feelings at being asked into a drawing room without curtains"

ceeded to improvise a free fantasia to express the horror of his feelings at being asked into a drawing room without curtains". Saint-Saëns was of course French. No such excuse for the German composer **Max Reger** who, at lunch here in 1909, knocked back four whiskies followed by twenty bottles of beer. Compared to theirs, **Frederick Delius**' month-long September visit in 1918 was comparatively normal; all that he required was for all of the clocks in the house to be allowed to run down as he could not stand the sound of ticking. Later visits to number 4 by **Leoš Janáček** and **Béla Bartók** were apparently unmarked by eccentricity. Henry Wood lived for another seven years after moving from Elsworthy Road. He died in Hitchin, Hertfordshire in 1944.

All that Delius required was for all of the clocks in the house to be allowed to run down as he could not stand the sound of ticking

- **AIR STUDIOS**, Lyndhurst Hall, Lyndhurst Road, NW3 (Tube: HAMPSTEAD) are not limited to classical recordings, but form an interesting companion piece to Abbey Road Studios (**see NW8**). In 1965 legendary record producer **George Martin** decided to leave Abbey Road where he had worked since 1950, in order to set up his own recording studios. Feeling that he had not been properly rewarded for his work with **The Beatles** he formed Associated Independent Recording (AIR) and took Abbey Road stalwarts **Peter Sullivan**, **John Burgess**, and **Ron Richards** with him to new premises in London's West End. With AIR, Martin paved the way for the freelance record producer who is hired by artists to produce them in his studio of choice. AIR has occupied the rather elegant Lyndhurst Hall premises since 1992 and it was designed very much with Martin's input. Previously a church and missionary school, the building was transformed into a state-of-the-art recording complex that has brought to this residential Hampstead street world-class facilities for film scoring, classical and orchestral work, rock and pop. Recent among the many scores recorded at Lyndhurst Hall include **Rachel Portman**'s soundtrack for *Chocolat* and **Hans Zimmer**'s music for *Hannibal*. George Martin, now retired, says that there was never any bitterness at his deserting the famous studio where he began his career. "Even after I left I was still welcomed back at Abbey Road and made to feel at home." Rather sadly, Martin's last personal project at AIR was an ill-judged celebrity-studded album of Beatles' numbers, *In My Life*, featuring among other distressing things, **Jim Carrey** singing 'I Am The Walrus'.

In 1965 legendary record producer George Martin decided to leave Abbey Road where he had worked since 1950, in order to set up his own recording studios

Boult attracted fame largely for the richness of his achievement, maintaining a low personal profile except when standing on the podium

Number **78 MARLBOROUGH MANSIONS**, Cannon Hill (Tube: WEST HAMPSTEAD) was the home of **Sir Adrian Cedric Boult** from 1966-1977. Born in Chester, Cheshire, he studied at Westminster School in London and then at Christ Church, Oxford under **Sir Hugh Percy Allen**, the influential organist and musical educator. He completed his training in Leipzig under the German composer and teacher **Johann Max(Imilian) Reger** and was inspired by seeing in action **Arthur Nikisch**, one of the 19th century's finest conductors. Returning to Britain, Boult gave concerts at Covent Garden and, in 1919, at the personal request of **Gustav Holst**, conducted the first performance of part of Holst's suite *The Planets*. From 1919-30 he taught at the Royal College of Music (**see SW7**) and was to become an internationally distinguished conductor. However, it was as Musical Director of the BBC (from 1930) and as its Conductor in Chief (1941) that he became a household name throughout Britain. After leaving the BBC he became director of the London Philharmonic Orchestra. Boult was a prominent figure of English musical life and a champion of English music at home and abroad. Unlike his extrovert contemporary **Sir Thomas Beecham**, Boult attracted fame largely for the richness of his achievement, maintaining a low personal profile except when standing on the podium. Towards the end of his life he wrote an autobiography, *My Own Trumpet* and a 1971 film about his conducting style, *Point Of The Stick*, took the name of an earlier book of his on conducting techniques. He lived to the age of 94 and died in Farnham, Kent.

- **ABBEY ROAD STUDIOS**
(Tube: ST JOHN'S
WOOD). In the 1920s,
when EMI was still The
Gramophone Company, its
recordings usually took
place in concert halls near
Oxford Circus, principally
Queen's Hall (**see The
Langham Hotel, W1**).
Custom-built studios were
unknown at the time, but

after much internal argument, the
company finally acquired and
developed number 3 Abbey Road, in
leafy St John's Wood, to create just
such a facility. Its birth was no easy
matter. **Trevor Osmond Williams**,
manager of The Gramophone
Company's Technical Recording
Department, championed the project
but met with strong resistance from
the artistic director of the HMV
division of the company who believed
it foolish for recording companies to
sink large sums of money into real
estate. Williams got his way, but
before the Abbey Road studio could
be opened he died unexpectedly at
the age of 45 of a brain tumour while
travelling in Austria. Meanwhile The
Gramophone Company merged with
Columbia to form EMI (Electrical &
Musical Industries, Ltd). The
opening ceremony in 1931 was
therefore intended to celebrate the
merger as well as the new facility. It
attracted a celebrity audience that
included **George Bernard Shaw** and
featured a performance of 'Land Of
Hope and Glory' by the London
Symphony Orchestra conducted by
Sir Edward Elgar. There is a photo-
graph of this ceremony where what
appears to be a shortage of chairs has
resulted in George Bernard Shaw
and the old Gramophone Company's
musical director sitting awkwardly on
the steps leading to the podium. So

The opening ceremony… featured a performance of 'Land Of Hope and Glory' by the London Symphony Orchestra conducted by Sir Edward Elgar

began the new life of an address that had enjoyed a colourful past in the 19th century and would become unimaginably famous in the twentieth. Back in July 1932 the 15-year-old **Yehudi Menuhin** recorded Elgar's *Violin Concerto* there, conducted by the composer. After a lifetime of association with Abbey Road's Studio One, Menuhin would conclude that its fine acoustics had not been achieved at a single stroke. "At one time they felt that sound had to be just pure sound, with no reverberations whatsoever," he recalled. "Then they went the other way and the room was dotted with loudspeakers all the way round so they would create echo effects that could be heard for miles around." But even before the outbreak of World War II, Abbey Road Studios became internationally famous among classical musicians. The subsequent list of artists who were to pass through is nothing less than a roll call of all-time great names. **Sir Thomas Beecham, Beniamino Gigli, John McCormack, Jascha Heifetz, Herbert von Karajan, Elisabeth Schwarzkopf, Ivor Novello, Paul Robeson, Sir Malcolm Sargent, André Previn, Kiri Te Kanawa, Placido Domingo** and **Mstislav Rostropovich** are just a few of the many who have recorded there. They would have been more than enough to give the premises a major reputation in the music business. However, Abbey Road also played host to famous jazz and light entertainment musicians such as **Fats Waller, Glenn Miller, Ella Fitzgerald, Ted Heath** and **Joe Loss** as well as a number of comedians. Eventually, of course, **The Beatles** would record there and title their final album *Abbey Road*, thus making an international shrine out of a north London recording studio.

The list of artists who were to pass through is nothing less than a roll call of all-time great names.

- Number **31 GROVE END ROAD** (Tube: ST JOHN'S WOOD) was one of the homes of **Sir Thomas Beecham**, conductor, impresario and one of British classical music's more roguish talents. The close proximity of this house to the Abbey Road Recording Studios was particularly amenable to Beecham and made him a frequent if not always punctual visitor there. "He would persistently arrive late for sessions," his widow recalled, "and…everybody would be out on the steps of Abbey Road waiting for him. Then he would casually discuss the weather or politics before walking slowly into the studio." Once inside, Beecham was quite likely to cause further confusion by changing his mind about what he was going to record or doing different parts from different works, making it hard for the engineers to get the balances right. On another occasion he met his match in piano virtuoso **Vladimir Horowitz** who, annoyed at the slow accompaniment conductor Beecham had provided during Tchaikovsky's *Piano Concerto No. 1*, suddenly set off at a gallop and left the maestro standing.

Beecham's temperament reflected the unique circumstances of his background. He was a man of independent means, the son of a wealthy business family (Beecham's Pills were a popular purgative) who was educated at Oxford and musically completely self-taught. From 1902 to 1904 he led a small operatic ensemble, then in 1906 established the New Symphony Orchestra in London. In 1910, financially supported by the family fortune, he took over the creative and business management of Covent Garden Opera

"He would persistently arrive late for sessions… everybody would be out on the steps of Abbey Road waiting for him. Then he would casually discuss the weather or politics before walking slowly into the studio."

House. He was the first in Britain to perform **Wagner**'s *Die Meistersinger von Nürnberg* and **Strauss**' *Elektra and Salome*, and was responsible for bringing to London such names as **Feodor Chalyapin**, **Wilhelm Furtwängler** and **Erich Kleiber**. In 1932 Beecham established the London Philharmonic Orchestra, before embarking on a protracted world tour. Upon his return to England he was rejected by The London Philharmonic as its sole manager but he responded in typically bullish fashion by founding, in 1932, Royal Philharmonic Orchestra which he managed until the end of his life. His intuitive approach to life was reflected both in his conducting style and in the many quotations attributed to him. He asserted that "Composers should write tunes that chauffeurs and errand boys can whistle." His most famous aphorism was "The English may not like music, but they absolutely love the noise it makes." His encounter with a woman in a non-smoking train compartment entered the folklore of The Great Western Railway. On lighting her cigarette she told Beecham, "I'm sure you won't object if I smoke." "Not at all," replied Beecham, "provided that you don't object if I'm sick." Towards the end of his life, Beecham and his wife moved to an apartment in Harley House, Marylebone Road. On hearing that colleague **Sir Malcolm Sargent** had regretfully predicted that the ailing Beecham would never again be seen at Abbey Road Studios, the invalid ordered a car to take him there forthwith and, sitting in his wheelchair in the control room, waited until Sargent had finished recording a **Gilbert & Sullivan** opera, before picking up the hand mike…

"I'm sure you won't object if I smoke." "Not at all," replied Beecham, "provided that you don't object if I'm sick."

- Number **45a ST JOHN'S WOOD HIGH STREET** (Tube: ST JOHN'S WOOD) is marked by plaque to commemorate the residence of **Benjamin Britten** who lived here between 1943 and 1946 following his return from the United States where he had been producing his large-scale instrumental works, the *Violin Concerto* and the *Sinfonia da Requiem*. While living here he worked on his first opera, *Peter Grimes*, which proved to be an immediate success. He later composed two grand scale operas: *Billy Budd* and *Gloriana*, the latter to celebrate the 1953 coronation of Queen Elizabeth. In addition to being a highly successful composer, Britten was also an accomplished pianist, often accompanying the tenor **Peter Pears**, in partnership with whom he and **Eric Crozier** founded in 1948 the annual Aldeburgh festival which was to see the premières of several of Britten's works. His remarkable career had begun early. At the age of 12 he began to study under the composer and teacher **Frank Bridge** (**see 4 Bedford Gardens, W8**). He later studied under **John Ireland** and **Arthur Benjamin** at the Royal College of Music (**see SW7**), subsequently working as a composer for radio, theatre and cinema, coming into close contact with the poet **W.H. Auden**. A few years after leaving this residence in the High Street he moved to number 59 at nearby Marlborough Place, where he remained until 1965. His last home was The Red House in Aldeburgh, Suffolk. In one of those awards that you feel might have been better timed, Britten was awarded a life peerage in the year of his death, 1976.

In one of those awards that you feel might have been better timed, Britten was awarded a life peerage in the year of his death, 1976

The post-war construction of **THE ROYAL FESTIVAL HALL**, South Bank (Tube: EMBANKMENT or WATERLOO) marked the start of a new era for this derelict waterfront area of Lambeth. For centuries the riverside tract had been dominated by grim factories and warehouses, but World War II bombings heavily damaged an area that had already been bought by the London County Council for development as a south side embankment. When in 1951 The Festival of Britain was mounted as a symbol of national regeneration and economic revival, the area was temporarily transformed with a number of futuristic or fanciful structures. Preparation was far from easy as the clay was so loose that in some places workmen had to dig nearly 20 metres to lay foundations. The Festival was to generate only one permanent building: The Royal Festival Hall, constructed on the old site of the Red Lion Brewery. Over the years other buildings would follow, to make up the entire South Bank Arts complex as it stands today. **The Queen Elizabeth Hall**, which seats about 1,000, and the smaller **Purcell Room** were opened in 1967 and these complement the Festival Hall as music venues suitable for recitals and chamber concerts. The Hayward Gallery, which opened in 1968, hosts art exhibitions and the National Theatre building (1976) includes three auditoriums (the Lyttelton, the Olivier, and the Cottesloe). Since 1990 The Royal Festival Hall has

The Festival [of Britain] was to generate only one permanent building: The Royal Festival Hall, constructed on the old site of the Red Lion Brewery

- been home to the London Philharmonic Orchestra and is in constant use for concerts, recitals and dance programmes. The orchestra, founded by **Sir Thomas Beecham** in 1932 (**see 31 Grove End Road, NW8**), has over the years featured principal conductors that include **Sir Adrian Boult**, **Sir John Pritchard**, **Bernard Haitink**, **Sir Georg Solti**, **Klaus Tennstedt** and **Franz Welser-Möst**. An organ, designed by **Ralph Downes**, makes a display of its functional construction and has exceptional clarity of tone. With seating capacity of around 3,000 The Festival Hall is one of London's premier venues for classical music, with sharp, clean acoustics but a reputation for being cold and impersonal that is hard to shake off. There remains something utilitarian about the auditorium, despite the major remodelling that took place in the 1990s.
- The Hall was originally designed by the London County Council architect Sir Robert Hogg Matthew in conjunction with J.L. Martin, Peter Moro and Edwin Williams at a cost of £2m. Although up and running for The Festival of Britain, it was not fully completed until 1965. Today the main enjoyment of the building still lies in its generous public spaces that, back in austere 1951, somehow managed to anticipate the current leisure tastes of concertgoers, with plenty of room for bars, meeting places, shops and restaurants.

The Festival Hall is one of London's premier venues for classical music, with sharp, clean acoustics but a reputation for being cold and impersonal that is hard to shake off

Number **4 ST JAMES'S PLACE** (Tube: PICCADILLY CIRCUS) bears a blue plaque that reads, "From this house, in 1848, Frederick Chopin 1810-1849 went to Guildhall to give his last public performance." This sets a suitably gloomy tone for a London visit that was indeed the end of the line for the Polish-French composer/pianist. The previous year **Frédéric Chopin**'s relationship with Amandine-Aurore-Lucile Dudevant, a.k.a. **George Sand**, had left him distraught. A wasting disease set in and this, combined with the downturn in his personal life, caused Chopin to go into general decline. Since his beloved Paris was in Revolutionary chaos he had little choice but to eke out a living in London through giving lessons and recitals. He took up residence at 4 St James's Place on 31st of October 1848, but stayed for only three weeks. From here on November 16th he travelled to the City of London Guildhall to give that last performance, one he was forced cut short due to his illness. He wrote home: "If I were well, with two lessons a day, I should have enough to live comfortably here but I'm weak: in three months, or four at the outside, I shall eat up what I have. I simply cannot breathe here; the climate is inconceivable for people in my state. We light the candles at 2 o'clock." He decided to swap "this hellish London" for Paris at whatever cost. Almost fittingly, as his train pulled out of London he suffered a seizure. He died on 17th October, 1849 in a Parisian apartment in Place Vendôme. He was 39 years old.

Chopin had little choice but to eke out a living in London through giving lessons and recitals

- **HER MAJESTY'S THEATRE**, Haymarket (Tube: PICCADILLY CIRCUS) is a theatre with a distinguished musical history, despite its current obligation to play seemingly indefinite host to **Andrew Lloyd Webber**'s *Phantom Of The Opera*. The original theatre on the site opened as an opera house (no phantom reported) in 1705. That building was the work of **Sir John Vanbrugh** who also designed Castle Howard in Yorkshire and Blenheim Palace in Oxfordshire. The Haymarket opera house was then known as The Queen's Theatre. Its first manager was the neoclassical dramatist **William Congreve** and in 1711 it staged **George Frederic Handel**'s *Rinaldo*, an occasion that prompted the composer's first trip to London (**see 25 Brook Street**, **W1**). Subsequently more than 20 Handel operas would be performed in London and the composer's second visit would become permanent. After a fire in 1789 the theatre was rebuilt and it was in this building (now rechristened The King's Theatre) in 1795 that the Austrian composer **Joseph Haydn** conducted his last three symphonies in circumstances that sound more than a little surreal. The works were performed from manuscript and had been written during his stay in London. At the première of Symphony No. 102 a chandelier fell into the middle of the auditorium during the finale. Since not a single member of the audience was injured, the cry of "Miracle! Miracle!" went up, although perhaps the audience might equally well have

At the première of Haydn's Symphony No. 102 *a chandelier fell into the middle of the auditorium during the finale*

cried out "Half-empty house! Half-empty house!" However, by some inexplicable process it was Haydn's *Symphony No. 96* that subsequently became known as the *Miracle Symphony*, while Haydn himself, when asked by his biographer about the plummeting light fitting, replied serenely "I know nothing about it." In 1816 further modifications were made to the theatre building by **John Nash**, the architect and city planner who also fashioned Regent Street, laid out Regent's Park and remodelled Brighton's Royal Pavilion. Upon reopening, the Haymarket theatre entered into a new phase. Among its 19th century productions were the first British performances of **Ludwig van Beethoven**'s *Fidelio* (1851), **Georges Bizet**'s *Carmen* (1878) and **Richard Wagner**'s *Der Ring des Nibelungen*. **Jenny Lind** also made her first British appearance here in 1847. Yet another structure was to replace The King's Theatre; the present Victorian Baroque-style building (at last, Her Majesty's Theatre!) was constructed in 1897 from designs by **C.J. Phipps** and **S. L. Florence**. Her Majesty's Theatre's fortunes in the 20th century were subsequently to fluctuate from 1920s performances of **Diaghilev** ballet through the first London performance of **Bernstein** and **Sondheim**'s *West Side Story* (1958), **Harnick** and **Bock**'s *Fiddler On The Roof*, **Peter Shaffer**'s *Amadeus* to, of course, the tenacious and inescapable *Phantom Of The Opera*.

- Number 180 **EBURY STREET** (Tube: VICTORIA or SLOANE SQUARE) was one of the several London locations where that peripatetic family the Mozarts lodged in 1764. Here eight-year old **Wolfgang Amadeus Mozart**, at the developmental stage when most children have difficulty getting the piano lid up without the help of an adult, wrote his first two symphonies, K16 and K19.

Today busy Ebury Street is hard to envisage as being on the fringes of a pastoral landscape, although that inveterate letter-writer Leopold, father of Wolfgang, identified the Ebury Street address as being in "Chelsea, near London", and also referred to it as a "spot outside town".

- Like so many musical visitors to London (or so it would seem from their gloomy correspondence), Leopold inevitably succumbed to illness (**see** his vivid commentary on the common cold in **19 Cecil Court, WC2**) and, depleted, had to be borne in a sedan chair to Ebury Street "in order to get more appetite and fresh strength from the good air". It must have worked, because Leopold was soon writing fulsomely of "one of the most beautiful views in the world" going on to add, "Wherever I turn my eyes I see gardens and in the distance the finest castles; and the house in which I am living has a lovely garden". Putting aside the unworthy suspicion that Leopold's turning eyes had lighted upon the gin, we can assume that bucolic Ebury Street both healed and mellowed him. From here the family moved to metropolitan Frith Street (**see W1**) before leaving the country.

Leopold, father of Wolfgang, identified the Ebury Street address as being in "Chelsea, near London"

On the corner of West Eaton Place is Number **99 EATON PLACE** (Tube: SLOANE SQUARE). This was where **Frédéric Chopin** gave his first public piano recital in Britain on June 23 1848. He was already in decline, although his illness was not yet as far advanced as when he gave his last British performance at The Guildhall in November of the same year. The impresario **Willert Beale** noted "In a drawing-room (Chopin) was to all a delight to hear, but in a larger space, before a more numerous audience, it gave more pain than pleasure. His appearance was so attenuated and his touch so enfeebled by long suffering". However, in elegant Eaton Square Chopin took pains that the audience should not be too numerous. "I had a select audience of 150 at one guinea, as I did not want to crowd the rooms" he said. "All the tickets were sold the day beforehand". Chopin, in London to escape the French Revolution, and friend to **Ferenc Liszt** and **Vincenzo Bellini**, had undeniable glamour, and one wonders if his consumptive pallor may not have further added to his Romantic appeal. In any case the Eaton Square recital was joyously received, even if some of the audience may have been privately disappointed not to experience something as weird and wonderful as the salon recital where Liszt and Chopin entered into a spirited pianoforte equivalent of 'Duelling Banjos' for nearly an hour, heedless of the fact that an errant moth had fallen into the lamp, leaving only the moonlight to illuminate their contest.

"In a drawing-room (Chopin) was to all a delight to hear, but in a larger space, before a more numerous audience, it gave more pain than pleasure"

- **MARLBOROUGH
- HOUSE**, Pall Mall (Tube:
- GREEN PARK) has been
- the site of many society
- occasions. **Ferenc Liszt** had
- dinner here with the **Prince
- of Wales** and **Princess
- Alexandra** on 11th April,
- 1886. Thirty-seven years
- later the Danish composer
- **Carl Nielsen** had tea here
- with the same Alexandra,
- by this time Queen Mother
- and one of the few High
- Society Danes available in
- London for Nielsen to talk
- to in his own language.

This was on June 29th 1923, Nielsen
having conducted a concert of his
works at Marlborough House the
night before. The *avant-garde*
Danish master was nearing the end
of his career, and from 1915 he had
been teaching at Copenhagen's Royal
Conservatory where he would later
become director. His London trip
seems to have been characterised by a
good deal of low comedy that makes
you wonder if Carl Nielsen could
possibly have been related to **Leslie
Nielsen** of Police Squad fame.
Coming to London equipped with
an English primer ("English in 100
Hours") he had found time to master
only two words: "ivory" and "yes".
This somewhat limited his conversation except when he was with the
Queen Mother. Not just a poor conversationalist but an absent-minded
packer as well, he forgot to bring a
suit and the one he borrowed was so
small that the trousers would not
fasten, obliging him to hold one hand
to his stomach at all times during the
Marlborough House tea party. All
went well until **Empress Dagmar of
Russia** turned up and required to be
escorted on the arm that was not
already being taken up by Alexandra.

*Not just a poor
conversationalist
but an absent-
minded packer as
well, he forgot to
bring a suit and
the one he
borrowed was so
small that the
trousers would
not fasten*

THE DIEUDONNÉ HOTEL once thrived in tiny Ryder Street, (Tube: GREEN PARK) although it is long gone and the site has been through various revisions since then. At one point it was The Eccentric Club but now seems to have been absorbed into exclusive chambers. When it was a hotel, one of the guests signing in on three separate occasions from 1888 to 1893 was **Pyotr Tchaikovsky**. His one previous visit had been as a tourist on which occasion he wrote his own version of the now standard letter penned by 19th century musicians visiting from abroad. "London" he wrote to his father, "makes a gloomy impression on the soul. You never see the sun and it rains at every step". During the first of his three stays at the Dieudonné in 1888 he conducted the British premiere of *Serenade for Strings*. On the 1889 visit he did the same for the *First Suite*. In 1893 it was for the first British performance of the *Fourth Symphony*. But enough of music—what really entranced Tchaikovsky was the weather. "Last year I enjoyed the fog daily" he wrote home, perhaps sarcastically or perhaps using "enjoyed" in the neutral sense of "experienced". He went on "But I never dreamed of the sort of thing we had today". It seems that after being hit by the routine pea-souper on his way to rehearsals in the morning, he was unprepared for a total eclipse by lunchtime. "When at midday I left St James's Hall…it was blackest night—as dark as a moonless autumn night at home".

"London" he wrote to his father, "makes a gloomy impression on the soul. You never see the sun and it rains at every step"

- **WESTMINSTER SCHOOL**, tucked away off The Sanctuary next to Westminster Abbey (Tube: WESTMINSTER) dates from The Reformation and was founded by Queen Elizabeth I in 1560. That kind of serious history makes for the sort of legends it is hard to disprove, so who is going to question whether Westminster's hall tables are really made from the timbers of the ships of the Spanish Armada? Perhaps they are, although the practice of making institutional furniture out of the enemy fleet seems an odd one. Ex-pupils of Westminster School

include a number of distinguished musical figures, not to mention **Sir Andrew Lloyd Webber**. In 1678 the headmaster **Dr Richard Busby** gave **Henry Purcell** a free place in the school. Purcell was a gangly 19 at the time, which perhaps took the edge off the award, although it did allow him, on a technicality, to become the only schoolboy ever to have been appointed organist at neighbouring Westminster Abbey, a post he took up in 1679 at the age of 20. In the 18th century **Charles Wesley** attended Westminster, later going on to publish a staggering 4,500 Methodist hymns and leaving another 3,000 in manuscript. **Sir Adrian Boult (see 76 Marlborough Mansions NW6)** attended Westminster before going on to study at Oxford and in Leipzig. The school now remembers him with a Music Scholarship bearing his name.

In 1678 the headmaster Dr Richard Busby gave Henry Purcell a free place in the school

Even judged by Chelsea's bohemian standards, Grainger was an memorably deranged artist, surrounded by rumour and myth, suspected of incest with his mother Rose

Australian-born composer and pianist **Percy Grainger** was something of a butterfly, living at a dozen different London addresses in the early 20th century before moving to the United States. Number **31a KING'S ROAD**, Chelsea (Tube: SLOANE SQUARE) held him for a record six years. Even judged by Chelsea's bohemian standards, Grainger was an memorably deranged artist, surrounded by rumour and myth, suspected of incest with his mother Rose (he denied this, claiming, perhaps unsatisfactorily, that he "treated her like a sister"), enthusiastically engaged in sado-masochistic relationship with **Karen Holten** and, in London, the object of near adulation by **Edvard Grieg** who called him "the wonderful Percy Grainger", noting in his diary on May 24th 1906 that he, Grieg, loved him "almost as if he were a young woman". Grainger himself had his first sexual experience in London (at 16 Cheyne Walk if you are really interested) with his patron, one **Mrs Lowery**. In between all this priapic activity Grainger managed to build a reputation as a brilliant concert pianist after arriving in London in 1901 from the conservatory in Frankfurt. It was under Grieg's influence that he began collecting and recording English folk songs in the form of wax-cylinder phono-graphs from which he was to make many famous arrangements. Grainger's original instrumental music includes *Handel in the Strand*, and *Mock Morris*. His folk-song arrangements for various groups of instruments include 'Early One Morning', 'Green Bushes', 'Molly on the Shore', 'Ye Banks and Braes' and 'Shepherd's Hey'. Some of these were also arranged for large wind ensembles. In the course of his folksy researches Grainger also formed friendships with other musical figures including **Herman Sandby**, **Frederick Delius**, **Cyril Scott** and **Balfour Gardiner**). He moved to the United States in 1914 and played for a few years with a U.S. Army band. Grainger was deeply affected by the suicide of his mother in 1922, returning to Australia alone in 1924 and touring there as a pianist, once in 1926 and again in 1934-35. In 1932 and 1933 he filled the post of Head of the Music Department at New York University and in 1935 he founded the Grainger Museum at Melbourne. This museum of Australian music still exists, preserving much of Grainger's own work as well as some of his artefacts, including his favoured terry-towelling clothing and a range of whips. A brave, or foolish, attempt to film his life story was made in 1999: *Passion*, with **Richard Roxburgh**, **Barbara Hershey** and **Emily Woof**.

He moved to the United States in 1914 and played for a few years with a U.S. Army band

The Victorians liked to think big but even they found that the original plan for a 30,000-capacity Kensington 'Coliseum' was rather too ambitious

Centrepiece of this musically rich area is **THE ROYAL ALBERT HALL** of Arts and Sciences… to give the building its full name (Tube: SOUTH KENSINGTON). It was essentially a grand memorial to **Prince Albert**, whose dream it had been to use the proceeds of The Great Exhibition of 1851 to set up a major cultural centre in the area. Under the direction of **Henry Cole**, the building was designed by an unconventional alliance of Royal Engineers, sculptors and craftsmen successively led by Captain Francis Fowke and General Henry Scott. The Victorians liked to think big but even they found that the original plan for a 30,000-capacity Kensington 'Coliseum' was rather too ambitious. They settled for a more modest design based on an elliptical Roman amphitheatre model with an original capacity of around 7,000. The Albert Hall's Italianate façade of red brick and terracotta bears an inspirational mosaic frieze inscribed: "This Hall was erected for the Advancement of the Arts and Sciences, and works of industry of all nations, in fulfilment of the intentions of Albert, Prince Consort". The auditorium is crowned by a 400-tonne dome raised above an arena, stalls, three tiers of boxes and gallery. Focus of the auditorium is the 9,000-pipe Willis organ, a majestic instrument that, when installed, was the largest known. The Hall has been an important venue for several British conductors, none more so than **Sir Malcolm Sargent**, a composer and organist who turned to conducting in the 1920s. He conducted the premiere of **Samuel Coleridge-Taylor**'s *Hiawatha* trilogy at the Hall in 1923, becoming asso-

ciated with the work and later turning its performance into an annual event. Inevitably though, The Albert Hall's fame as a classical venue rests upon its long association with the Promenade Concerts. These concerts are so called because they were always intended for a non-seated audience that would stand or mill around—a format already explored in London by **Louis Jullien** and **Michael Balfe**. The concerts began in 1895 when they were held at Queen's Hall (**see Abbey Road Studios, NW8**). From the start they were conducted by **Henry Wood** whose name is now permanently associated with "The Proms" which he conducted for half a century. When Queen's Hall was flattened by a Second World War bomb, the concerts moved to this hall where they are still staged annually from July to September. Their success had a considerable influence on English musical life, mainly because of their broad appeal, established by Wood. Originally they encompassed the entire range of 18th and 19th century orchestral music but later introduced the works of contemporary figures like **Richard Strauss**, **Claude Debussy** and **Arnold Schoenberg**. Now a major world music festival, The Proms always culminate in a famous Last Night which has become a ritualistic celebration with unsettling chauvinistic overtones as Union flags are waved and 'Land of Hope and Glory' is loudly sung by a swaying crowd. The Albert Hall is a Grade I listed building, an acknowledgment of its outstanding architectural importance. At the time of writing, a comprehensive building development and restoration programme is underway and scheduled for completion in 2003.

The Proms always culminate in a famous Last Night which has become a ritualistic celebration with unsettling chauvinistic overtones

Malcolm Sargent assumed for himself the mantle of Britain's "ambassador of music" as he toured the world

Sir Malcolm Sargent

Number **9 ALBERT HALL MANSIONS**, Kensington Gore (Tube: SOUTH KENSINGTON) was home to the conductor **Sir Malcolm Sargent** for the last twenty years of his life. In the 1930s Sargent had lived at 12 Wetherby Place, also in SW7, in a house he briefly rented to **Arthur Schnabel** while he was forced to remove himself to Switzerland to recuperate from severe illness. Harold Malcolm Watts Sargent, to give him his full name, assumed for himself the mantle of Britain's "ambassador of music" as he toured the world, having earned his diploma from the Royal College of Organists at the age of 16 and become England's youngest doctor of music in his early twenties. His debut was in 1921, when he conducted his own composition with **Henry Wood**'s Queen's Hall Orchestra, and in 1923 he joined the staff of the Royal College of Music (**see Royal College of Music** also **SW7**). **Sir Thomas Beecham** enlisted his help in the formation of the London Philharmonic in 1932 (**see 31 Grove End Road, NW8**) and subsequent posts he held were with the Hallé Orchestra (until 1942), the Liverpool Philharmonic (until 1948), and the BBC Symphony Orchestra (until 1957). Sargent was knighted in 1947 and took over The Henry Wood Promenade Concerts from 1948 until his death, here, close by The Royal Albert Hall that had been the site of so many of his successes.

- Number **39 HAR-RINGTON GARDENS**, (Tube: GLOUCESTER ROAD or SOUTH KENSINGTON) was the memorable London house that **Sir William Schwenk Gilbert** created for himself. Apart from being **Sir Arthur Sullivan**'s ideal librettist (if uneasy professional partner), Gilbert was a man with a remarkable visual imagination; he was a decent illustrator, a good draughtsman and, as this lively piece of architecture suggests, no mean designer either. Gilbert supplied the concept and the architectural practice of **Sir Ernest George** and **Harold Ainsworth Peto** provided the professional services.

- George and Peto specialised in expensive domestic architecture, favouring brick with terracotta dressings. They made quite an impression on this district of London with a style derived from North European late Gothic and Renaissance architecture. Their houses for the Cadogan Estate, particularly those in Chelsea's Pont Street, gave rise to a minor architectural label: Pont Street Dutch.

W.S. Gilbert

Gilbert was an extraordinary man who started out as a rather facetious writer and satirist but soon developed a genuinely witty style lampooning contemporary behaviour. Even if the topicality of much of his burlesque is long lost, at his best Gilbert was so good as to transcend his targets.

Detail of main entrance

Matching Sullivan's music artfully, Gilbert managed to structure his words in musical shapes and allow Sullivan the parallel opportunity to mock the musical conventions of the day. An energetic and productive man, Gilbert conducted himself as the very model of an enlightened Edwardian gentleman. His life was bracketed by two odd events: being kidnapped by Italian bandits at the age of two (he was released for a ransom) and succumbing to a fatal heart attack at the age of seventy-five after rescuing a woman from drowning in a lake on his country estate in Harrow Weald, northwest of London. He had been teaching her to swim, although it seems not well enough. As a young man he had thought of a legal career and an inheritance in 1861 enabled him to leave his civil service job to pursue it. He was called to the bar in 1863, but he had already begun to contribute comic verse to periodicals and his dramatic career took off when he was recommended as someone who could knock out a bright Christmas piece in only two weeks. He responded with *Dulcamara, or the Little Duck and the Great Quack*, a success that quickly brought other commissions. In 1870 Gilbert met Sullivan, and the rest, as they say, is history. At his exuberant Harrington Gardens home where he resided from 1883 to 1890, Gilbert wrote *Princess Ida, The Mikado, Ruddigore, The Yeomen Of The Guard* and *The Gondoliers*.

Matching Sullivan's music artfully, Gilbert managed to structure his words in musical shapes and allow Sullivan the parallel opportunity to mock the musical conventions of the day

- **THE ROYAL COLLEGE OF**
- **MUSIC**, Prince Consort Road
- (Tube: SOUTH KENSINGTON).
- Normally The Royal College of
- Music is visible and accessible from
- the back of The Royal Albert Hall,
- down a flight of steps
- and beyond yet
- another a memorial
- to Victoria and
- Albert. Renovation
- work has for some
- time blocked off this
- approach and vista,
- and at the time of
- writing the college is
- still only accessible
- from Prince Consort
- Road. It was founded
- in 1882 by the Prince
- of Wales and its first
- director was **Sir**
- **George Grove**, today
- remembered chiefly

for his multi-volume dictionary of music and musicians. A writer and not a musician himself, Grove was an interesting first choice for director. He had begun as a civil engineer and from 1856 to 1896 wrote analytical notes for the Crystal Palace concerts, establishing benchmarch standards for programme commentary. In 1867 he visited Vienna with **Sir Arthur Sullivan** and discovered the manuscripts for **Schubert**'s *Rosamunde*. Grove was succeeded in the post by several distinguished men including **Sir Charles Hubert Parry (see 17 Kensington Square, W8)** and the college's student roll call has included **Gustav Holst**, **Ralph Vaughan Williams**, **Benjamin Britten**, **Michael Tippett** and **Samuel Coleridge-Taylor**. Coleridge-Taylor was of particular interest, rising from a poor upbringing in London's East End by virtue of unstoppable talent. At the

The college's student roll call has included Gustav Holst, Ralph Vaughan Williams, Benjamin Britten, Michael Tippett and Samuel Coleridge-Taylor

Here is the oldest surviving string keyboard, a clavicytherium, something that is probably easier to play than pronounce

age of five he began playing the violin and joined the choir of a Presbyterian church in Croydon, where **H.A. Walters** guided his progress and arranged his admittance to the Royal College of Music in 1890. The first black British composer (he was the son of a West African father and an English mother), Coleridge-Taylor was championed by **Sir Edward Elgar** who once wrote an emotional letter to the committee of the Three Choirs Festival in Gloucester, begging them to give Coleridge-Taylor a commission. "He still wants recognition", wrote Elgar, "and is far and away the cleverest fellow amongst the young men. Please don't…throw away the chance of doing a good act!"

The college maintains a Museum of Instruments, mainly antique. Among the star exhibits are **Haydn**'s clavichord and Handel's spinet. Here too is the oldest surviving string keyboard, a clavicytherium, something that is probably easier to play than pronounce. There is also a collection of historical portraits of leading musicians. Today The Royal College of Music has a staff of over 200, with five ensembles in residence, numerous visiting professors and a list of musicians of international standing – the Prince Consort Professors – who visit and teach on an occasional basis. Every term there are visits from other performers, teachers, composers, conductors and scholars who contribute to the College's workshop, masterclass and lecture programmes.

Number **7 SYDNEY PLACE**, (Tube: SOUTH KENSINGTON) played host to the Hungarian composer **Béla Bartók** while he was performing in London in 1933. A blue plaque celebrates the occasion he stayed here, the guest of **Duncan Wilson**, although Bartók also seems to have favoured some other southwest London addresses with his presence. In the 1920s he was a frequent visitor to 10

Netherton Grove in SW10, the home of the violinist **Adila Fachiri**. A man of consistent tastes, he also paid frequent calls upon another female violinist, the divertingly named **Jelly d'Arányi** who lived at 18 Elm Park Gardens in SW10. However it was the plaque-worthy 1933 visit during which Bartók and **Adrian Boult** (**see 78 Marlborough Mansions, NW6**) gave the first British performance of his Second Piano Concerto. Bartók returned to London in 1936 when he met **Paul Hindemith**, and then made two more visits in 1938 during the second of which he played, together with his wife **Ditta Pásztory** (a pianist, not, as one might have reasonably hazarded, a violinist) the British première of his Sonata for Two Pianos and Percussion. By the end of the 1930s his native Hungary appeared to be in danger of capitulation to the Nazis, and Bartók found it impossible to remain there. After a second concert tour of the United States in 1940, he emigrated there later the same year.

A man of consistent tastes, he also paid frequent calls upon another female violinist, the divertingly named Jelly d'Arányi

Number **15 GLOUCESTER WALK**, (Tube: HIGH STREET KENSINGTON or NOTTING HILL GATE). **Jean Sibelius** visited England four times in all, between 1905 and 1912. In 1909 he resided here, just off Kensington Church Street. These trips, along with one to the U.S., seemed to coincide both with greater international acceptance of his music and a profound change of register in the Finnish composer's long life. (**Johannes Brahms** was 32 years old when Sibelius was born; 22-year old **Elvis Presley** would record 'Jailhouse Rock' in the year that he died). When he began visiting Britain, Sibelius had

already enjoyed a long career in music after being much influenced by **Pyotr Tchaikovsky**. He had explored 19th century Romanticism and expressed a fiercely passionate nationalism in works like *The Karelia Suite* and *Finlandia*. His long final phase was to produce comparatively little work. In 1904 he had bought a plot of land outside Helsinki and built a house in which he was to live for the rest of his life with his wife and daughters. Here he was soberly isolated from the temptations of the city where, as can so often be the case in gelid Finland, his fondness for warming alcohol had at one point turned into a worrying tendency to fall over a lot. Despite having a national day named after him on his 50th birthday, Sibelius suffered a crisis of confidence and published no music at all during the last thirty years of his life.

Despite having a national day named after him on his 50th birthday, Sibelius suffered a crisis of confidence and published no music at all during the last thirty years of his life

- Number **4 BEDFORD GARDENS** (Tube: HOLLAND PARK) was the London home of the highly influential English composer, virtuoso viola player and conductor **Frank Bridge**. A blue plaque high on the house wall attests to this, for those with good eyesight.

Undoubtedly one of the most accomplished musicians of his day, Sussex-born Bridge was known especially for his chamber music and songs. He studied under **Sir Charles Villiers Stanford** at The Royal College of Music (**see SW7**), beginning with the violin but soon changing to viola. After a spell with the **Joachim Quartet** in 1906 he played with the **English String Quartet** until 1915 and held various positions as a conductor, both symphonic and operatic. Bridge composed in many genres, but seemed to find his greatest contemporary success with smaller forms, such as his 1910 *Phantasie Quartet* for piano and strings, several string quartets and assorted piano pieces. His early works were Romantic but gradually he moved toward atonality. In fact Bridge was one of the first British musicians to recognise the merits of the Austrian composer **Alban Berg** who was an early proponent of the atonal style. Although Bridge's compositions are very rarely heard today, his impact as a teacher was considerable, and his influence on his many pupils was profound, never more so than in the case of **Benjamin Britten** (**see 45a St John's Wood High Street, NW8**) who first came to public attention with his 1937 piece *Variations on a Theme by Frank Bridge*.

Although Bridge's compositions are very rarely heard today, his impact as a teacher was considerable, and his influence on his many pupils was profound, never more so than in the case of Benjamin Britten

A youthful prodigy, Clementi had already composed an oratorio by the age of twelve

Muzio Clementi

KENSINGTON CHURCH STREET is a residential street famed for its antique shops (Tube: NOTTING HILL GATE or KENSINGTON HIGH STREET). At number 128 is a house with a blue plaque marking the residency of the Italian-born English pianist and composer **Muzio Clementi** (1750-1832), the so-called "father of the piano". A youthful prodigy, Clementi had already composed an oratorio by the age of twelve. In 1766 **Peter Beckford** brought the boy to England to live in Wiltshire where he pursued his studies. At the age of 23 Clementi made his first foray to London where met with immediate success as both a pianist and a composer. He made brilliant use of the piano, a relatively new instrument at the time, and from 1777 to 1780 was employed as harpsichordist by the Italian Opera in London. In 1780 he went on tour visiting Vienna, Munich, Strasbourg and Paris, but in 1782 returned to London, where for the next 20 years he was simultaneously teacher (his pupils included **Johann Baptist Cramer**, **Giacomo Meyerbeer**, and **John Field**), composer and performer. In 1799 he co-founded a firm for both music publishing and the manufacture of pianos opening a piano store in Tottenham Court Road in 1811. In his later years he devoted himself to composition, much of it undertaken in the period when he occupied 128 Kensington Church Street.

His lasting fame depends on his innovation of piano technique, his piano sonatas and his celebrated studies for piano, the *Gradus ad Parnassum*.

- Number **17 KENSINGTON SQUARE** (Tube: HIGH STREET KENSINGTON) was home to **Sir Charles Hubert Parry**, composer, writer, and teacher, and an influential force in the revival of English music towards the end of the 19th century. In London in 1877 Parry visited a distinguished visitor to the capital, **Richard Wagner**. Richard and Cosima Wagner were staying for a month at 12 Orme Square with **Edward Dannreuther**, unsuccessfully trying to raise money for Cosima's cash-strapped Bayreuth Festivals. Parry visited them twice in May, on the second occasion noting that Wagner "was in great fettle and talked to an open-mouthed group in brilliant fashion". Cosima's rather less gracious assessment recorded in her diary states "R. annoyed at the visitors". In 1883 Parry was appointed festival conductor of the University of Oxford and also joined the staff of the Royal College of Music, (**see SW7**) becoming its director in 1894. In 1900 he became professor of music at Oxford; he was knighted in 1898 and created a baronet in 1903. It was at this Kensington Square address that he wrote his *Symphonic Variations* plus assorted hymns (including 'Repton' and 'England') and several anthems. One of these was his "national anthem" for Newfoundland, (a territory with a complex history although surely one that never included nationhood) and his best known anthem, 'Jerusalem'. This stirring setting of words from William Blake's *Milton* became Britain's informal national anthem during World War I. To this day its rousing nationalism is still tapped whenever piety, patriotism or alcohol gains the upper hand.

An influential force in the revival of English music towards the end of the 19th century

Sir Charles Hubert Parry

On the corner of Holland Street and Hornton Street (Tube: HIGH STREET KENSINGTON) is number **56 HORNTON STREET**, once the home of **Sir Charles Villiers Stanford** who lived here between 1894 and 1916. The very English-sounding name belied the Irish roots of a composer, conductor and teacher born in Dublin in 1852 who was greatly to influence the next generation of British composers and who taught **Ralph Vaughan Williams**, **Sir Arthur Bliss** and **Gustav Holst**. Stanford studied at Trinity College, Dublin and Queen's College, Cambridge, then in Leipzig with **Karl Reinecke** and **Friedrich Kiel** in Berlin. He became professor of composition at the Royal College of Music (**see SW7**) in 1883 and professor of music at Cambridge in 1887. While living at this address he composed his *Fifth* and *Sixth Symphonies*, his *Second Piano Concerto* and a whole slew of Irish rhapsodies and song cycles, plus an opera entitled *Shamus O'Brien*. **Pyotr Tchaikovsky** visited him here (Stanford noted that he looked like "an ambassador") as did **Charles-Camille Saint-Saëns** and **Max Bruch**, who is remembered by the world for his *Violin Concerto in G Minor* and by Stanford for resembling "a storekeeper from the Middle West". Stanford moved from Hornton Street to 9 Lower Berkeley Street (now Fitzhardinge Street, W1) where he died in March of 1924. He is buried in Westminster Abbey.

Max Bruch, who is remembered by the world for his Violin Concerto in G Minor *and by Stanford for resembling "a storekeeper from the Middle West"*

Number **22 ALFRED PLACE**, (Tube: GOODGE STREET) on the fringes of Bloomsbury, is where **Gustav Mahler** stayed on his only trip to Britain in the summer of 1892. He was in London to conduct eighteen performances of opera (**see Royal Opera House, WC2**) including *Der Ring des Nibelungen*, *Tristan und Isolde*, *Tannhäuser* and *Fidelio*. At the start of his visit he stayed at Keyser's Royal

Hotel (now demolished) 69 Torrington Square, later moving to rooms in nearby Alfred Place. History has painted a somewhat unconvivial portrait of this Austrian-Jewish composer and conductor, alienated from his father and with a mother fixation was so profound as to make him walk with a slight limp in unconscious imitation of her disability. Add to this an unremitting catalogue of childhood illness and death among his eleven siblings plus a congenitally weak heart inherited from his mother, and it hardly comes as a surprise that Mahler was not known for his sunny disposition. It is something of a surprise therefore to learn that for his sole London trip he made a touchingly diligent attempt to learn English, paying particular attention to the pages in the phrase book to do with the theatre. He impressed everyone as a remarkably unassuming man disinclined to talk about his own compositions, and **Herman Klein** observed "his efforts to speak English, even with those who spoke German fluently, were untiring as well as amusing". However Klein felt obliged to add that Mahler's linguistic efforts "tended to prolong conversation".

It hardly comes as a surprise that Mahler was not known for his sunny disposition

In 1899 number **126 SOUTHAMPTON ROW** (Tube: RUSSELL SQUARE) was a baker's shop. In the flat above, on December 2nd, was born **Giovanni Battista Barbirolli** the son of Lorenzo Barbirolli, a well-regarded Italian violinist. Giovanni would become John, and John would become Sir John in a long and distinguished musical career that was to link his name forever with Manchester's **Hallé Orchestra**. Young Barbirolli, something of a prodigy, was taught to play the violin but changed to the cello at the age of seven, entered London's Trinity College of Music at ten and transferred to the Royal Academy of Music (**see NW1**) at twelve. In 1916, he became the youngest member of Henry Wood's Queen's Hall Orchestra and in 1917 gave his first solo cello recital in London. After a spell in the army he began playing in the London Symphony Orchestra in 1919 and then in Thomas Beecham's Covent Garden Orchestra (**see WC2**). In 1921 at an early performance of the work he was the soloist in **Sir Edward Elgar**'s *Cello Concerto*. Subsequent appointments included conductorships with the Hallé Orchestra, Manchester (1943-68), where he gained international recognition as a conductor, and in Texas for the Houston Symphony Orchestra (1961-67). A decade of declining health did not prevent him from worldwide guest conducting, recording and touring with major orchestras. He suffered a fatal heart attack in London in 1970, at 45 Huntsworth Mews, NW1. He was the same age as the century and died less than three miles away from the room where he was born.

Giovanni would become John, and John would become Sir John in a long and distinguished musical career that was to link his name forever with Manchester's Hallé Orchestra

Sir John Barbirolli

- The present **TAVISTOCK HOUSE**, Tavistock Square (Tube: EUSTON or EUSTON SQUARE) is not the original, but the location was once the home of **Charles Dickens**. From 1871 to 1874, **Charles-François Gounod**, the French composer of operas, was the guest of its then owner, the singer **Georgina Weldon**. Eventually Gounod's fame would rest on his most successful opera *Faust*, but despite pursuing a distinguished career in Rome, Vienna and Paris, the composer, whose 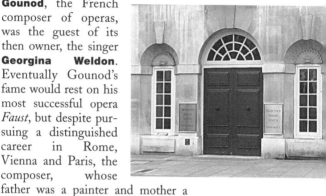 father was a painter and mother a pianist, possessed a somewhat passionate temperament that was more than once given expression at this Bloomsbury address. He seemed to have an natural taste for the vivid – two of his earliest operas were entitled *Sapho* and *La Nonne Sanglante* (The Bloody Nun). Despite being championed by **Hector Berlioz**, who had given him his early training, these works were not well received. During his sojourn at Tavistock House Gounod proved himself to be a passionate if not unhinged guest. On more than one occasion he engaged in what sound like Tarantino-esque wrestling bouts with Georgina Weldon on the floor, scrabbling for possession not of a gun but of some manuscript he wanted to burn and she to save. Not that there was a total absence of firearms, since Gounod also purchased a revolver while in London, perhaps in order to feel more secure when he indulged in one of his fitful nocturnal rambles around the streets of Bloomsbury, clad only in a nightshirt and emitting weird cries.

On more than one occasion he engaged in what sound like Tarantino-esque wrestling bouts with Georgina Weldon on the floor

CORAM'S FIELDS (Tube: RUSSELL SQUARE) at the northern end of Lamb's Conduit Street, ought to be a pleasant green space, but these days it succeeds only in looking rather scrappy. Visually it is no match for pleasant Brunswick Square that adjoins its western side. Coram's Fields is the present site of the Foundling Hospital founded by **Captain Thomas Coram** in 1741 as a refuge for abandoned children. Coram's beneficent gesture was generously supported by **George Frederic Handel** and the hospital headquarters consequently became rich in Handel-related items. Although the current location is in part a mock up of the original building that first stood in Brunswick Square, the artefacts and art pieces within (the artist **William Hogarth** was another benefactor) are originals. There are two portraits of Handel and a bust of him by **Louis-François Roubiliac**. Of particular interest is the keyboard of the original hospital chapel organ, an instrument that was presented by Handel. This is of the type where the familiar black and white identification of the keys is reversed, as it was in the days of harpsichords and spinettes. The keyboard has three manuals, one of three octaves, two of four and a half octaves, and the instrument to which it belonged was once played by Handel at a performance of *The Messiah*. A fair copy of *The Messiah* also belongs to the hospital, as do the scores of the *Foundling Hospital Anthem*, written specially for the organisation by the composer.

Of particular interest is the keyboard of the original hospital chapel organ, an instrument that was presented by Handel

The **SAVOY HOTEL**, The Strand (Tube: EMBANKMENT or CHARING CROSS). The Savoy Hotel was built in 1889 by **Richard D'Oyly Carte**, entrepreneur, theatre manager and amateur building designer. He had conceived the hotel very much in a spirit of theatricality and celebrity – a luxurious and glamorous companion piece to his adjacent Savoy Theatre. He introduced the brand new phenomenon of electric lighting as a symbol of modernity to both establishments, and from the start there were musical associations with the hotel as well as the theatre. Once **Johann Strauss the Elder** was seen to lead the hotel orchestra. On another occasion **Anna Pavlova** took something of a risk with her ballet career by appearing in the cabaret. **Giacomo Puccini** entertained Australian opera star **Dame Nellie Melba** after the opening night of *Manon Lescaut* and it was in her honour too that The Savoy chef devised and named the now famous sweet, Peach Melba. In a less classical vein the theatre even had its own house band, The Savoy Orpheans, who achieved national fame through their late night BBC radio broadcasts. The Savoy Theatre next door, opened eight years before the hotel, had done what it had been built to do supremely well: it had given a home to the wildly popular operettas of **William S. Gilbert** and **Arthur Sullivan**. From the opening production of *Patience* through *Iolanthe*, *The Mikado*, *The Yeomen of the Guard* and *The Gondoliers*, the Savoy operas, as they were known, proved immensely popular and are still enthusiastically performed all over the world. However *The Gondoliers* marked the beginning of the end of the famous Gilbert and Sullivan partnership. Neither had ever been comfortable

From the start there were musical associations with the hotel as well as the theatre

Dame Nellie Melba

Soon Gilbert wrote an historic note to Sullivan: "The time for putting an end to our collaboration has at last arrived…"

with the other's fame and the split, although apparently triggered by the contentious cost of a carpet for the Savoy (the theatre's expenses were to be shared equally by Gilbert, Sullivan and D'Oyly Carte) was more probably an inevitable consequence of long and deep rivalry. The carpet provided the excuse and the rift was permanent. Soon Gilbert wrote an historic note to Sullivan: "The time for putting an end to our collaboration has at last arrived… in point of fact, after the withdrawal of The Gondoliers, our united work will be heard in public no more." Famous last words.

The **EMBANKMENT GARDENS** (Tube: EMBANKMENT) form a narrow strip of public park between Waterloo and Hungerford bridges near The Savoy Hotel. Due to the strong links between The Savoy and the operettas of Gilbert and Sullivan, this was of course the logical place to locate a bust of **Sir Arthur Seymour Sullivan**. If the location is appropriate, the memorial is perhaps less so. Although it was Sullivan's librettist **William. S. Gilbert** who came over as the worldly and incisive one, Sullivan too could display drollness and irony, as **Charles-Camille Saint-Saëns** testified: "Sullivan was as much a satirist in musical notes as Gilbert in the verbal test.

Their repartees in collaboration often reminded of the sarcasms of Voltaire." What then would these iconoclastic musical partners have made of this sentimental memorial? Its pedestal bears one of Gilbert's duller verses (Is life a boon?/If so it must befal/ That death, whene'er he call/Must call too soon) and Sullivan's bust is kitchily attended by a topless Muse on her knees, her mandolin flung aside. In fact the final years of Sullivan's life had little to do with Edwardian romance. Alienated from his old partner, he spent his declining years living dissolutely in Monte Carlo, lost in a haze of morphine, fighting a losing battle with bronchitis. Eventually he returned to London and died in the winter of 1900. Gilbert, on the Continent, learned of his former collaborator's death in the newspaper. Their old colleague **Richard D'Oyly Carte** was so ill that no one told him of Sullivan's demise although from his sickbed he saw the funeral cortège pass his window anyway.

Its pedestal bears one of Gilbert's duller verses… and Sullivan's bust is kitchily attended by a topless Muse on her knees, her mandolin flung aside

Number **31 KING STREET**, Covent Garden (Tube: COVENT GARDEN) was where **Thomas Arne** grew up. One of British music's more colourful characters, Arne was born in London in March 1710, the son of an upholsterer-cum-undertaker of this address. Although educated at Eton and intended for the law, he secretly practised both violin and keyboard instruments, becoming so proficient as to defuse all parental objections to a musical career. He was largely self-taught, simultaneously developing his musical tastes and saving his money by going to the local opera dressed in a footman's livery in order to gain free admission. Legend has it that the young Arne would practise with his music propped up on one of the coffins belonging to the funereal side of his father's oddly twinned business. Matter-of-fact about death, he was enthusiastic about sex, and when in 1735 he moved to nearby Great Queen Street, it was popularly assumed that this was because it placed him nearer to Drury Lane's prostitutes. Certainly one of his pupils noted "He never could pass by a woman in the street, to the end of his life, without concupiscence or, in plain English, picking her up". The pupil went on grimly "It has frequently happened in walking home with my wife of a night, if we have by some accident been separated for a few minutes, that she has been accosted by the Doctor with that design". As a young man Arne taught both his sister, later to become famous as the actress **Mrs. Cibber**, and his young brother to sing, and they both appeared in Arne's first opera, *Rosamond*.

Although educated at Eton and intended for the law, he secretly practised both violin and keyboard instruments

- The **ROYAL OPERA HOUSE**, Covent Garden (Tube: COVENT GARDEN). The Royal Opera House has been located at its present site in Covent Garden since 1732 when the first Theatre Royal opened. Since then there have existed three successive theatres and in 1946 the Royal Ballet and the Royal Opera were established as resident companies. Although The Royal Opera House is one of the world's most famous venues, its rich past has to some extent been temporarily eclipsed by its disaster-prone present. Opera lovers addicted to melodramatic plots of loss, betrayal, and revenge no longer had to wait for the actual productions to be mounted: boardroom struggles, firings and bitter accusations have provided a visceral drama that makes traditional blood-soaked Italian opera look like the Teletubbies. An ill-judged fly-on-the-wall BBC TV documentary only

made matters worse. However, the theatre's past was not always plain sailing either. The opening performance back in 1732 was of **William Congreve**'s comedy *The Way of the World*, and this was quickly followed by a revival of *The Beggar's Opera*. For the next 150 years Italian opera dominated, although the theatre also accommodated the first performances of several works by **George Frederic Handel** and indeed staged the first London performance of his Messiah in 1743. It was from this performance that came the tradition of standing during the 'Hallelujah Chorus': King George II did it and, naturally, so did everyone else. The theatre burned down in 1808 to be replaced by another which suffered the same fate 48 years later. Its replacement was the present building. In the early 19th century under the management of **Charles**

Its rich past has to some extent been temporarily eclipsed by its disaster-prone present

On the morning of September 17, 2000, she was discovered dead in bed

Kemble, the music of **Carl Maria von Weber** became fashionable and his *Der Freischütz* was performed 53 times at The Royal Opera House. Kemble commissioned a new opera from von Weber and in return got *Oberon*, another success, although it was von Weber's last work; he died during its production (**see 103 Great Portland Street, W1**). Covent Garden is also associated with some notable women singers. It saw the début of **Maria Malibran** and the first British performance of **Giulia Grisi** whose success reinforced the popularity of Italian opera. The teenaged **Adelina Patti** filled Grisi's shoes when she retired and soon attracted a major following of her own. Perhaps the most famous Royal Opera débutante was the Australian Helen Porter Mitchell, a.k.a. **Nellie Melba**. In 1888, singing the title role in **Gaetano Donizetti**'s *Lucia di Lammermoor*, she began a 38-year association with The Royal Opera House. Under the management of Augustus Harris in the latter part of the 19th century, German opera began to rival the Italian product (which at one point had caused a temporary name change to The Royal Italian Opera). **Gustav Mahler** conducted a German opera company's productions of **Wagner**'s *Der Ring des Nibelungen* and *Tristan*. Later an English language version of the *Ring Cycle* would signal the start of a gradual process of democratisation of the Opera House's repertoire. During World War II the place became a Mecca dance hall, a startling conversion that prompted music publishers Boosey & Hawkes to buy the lease. With the formation of the Covent Garden Opera Trust the broad framework of today's subsidised Royal Opera was finally established.

- Number **19 CECIL COURT** (Tube:
- LEICESTER SQUARE was where
- **Wolfgang Amadeus Mozart** and his
father, mother and sister
lodged with a barber, **John
Couzin** between April 24th
and August 6th 1764. This
was prior to the family's
move to Frith Street (**see
20 Frith Street, W1**) and
followed a single night spent
at a hostelry called The
White Bear (now demol-
ished) in Piccadilly. Almost
at once Wolfgang's father
Leopold became consumed

by the burning topic that seems to
have obsessed all 18th and 19th
century visitors to London. "In
England there is a kind of native
complaint, which is called a *cold*" he
wrote home darkly, revealing a bib-
lical taste for italics. "That is why you
hardly ever see people wearing
summer clothes," he continued.
"This so-called *cold*, in the case of
people who are not constitutionally
sound, becomes so dangerous that in
many instances it develops into a *consumption*, as they call it here." New to
the phenomenon as he was, and
despite coming from a non-medical
background in architecture and
bookbinding, Leopold was not above
offering a snap diagnosis. "The wisest
course for such people to adopt is to
leave England and cross the sea," he
advised. "Many examples can be
found of people recovering their
health on leaving this country. I
caught this *cold*…" In another letter
home the Mozart paterfamilias suddenly becomes a fashion corre-
spondent. "In London everybody
seems to be in fancy dress," he wrote.
"You cannot imagine what my wife
and my little girl look like in English
hats, and I and our big Wolfgang in
English clothes."

*"In England there
is a kind of native
complaint, which
is called a
cold…that is why
you hardly ever see
people wearing
summer clothes*

MANZI's RESTAURANT

(Tube: LEICESTER SQUARE) in Leicester Street, just off Leicester Square, was once the Hôtel Du Commerce. It was there that **Johann Strauss The Elder** stayed on his 1838 visit to London. He had booked rooms at another hotel, in Fleet Street, which he left almost at once deeming them unsatisfactory, with the result that he was taken to court for non-payment and threatened with debtor's prison. Since by now all his money had been stolen as well, Strauss might have been forgiven for fleeing the country, but after the publisher **Robert Cocks** discharged his debts, the Viennese waltzmeister decided to stay. On this London trip he led an orchestra at numerous concerts and balls, taking the opportunity to introduce at Buckingham Palace a new waltz with the tactical if less than catchy title of 'Homage to Queen Victoria of Great Britain'. Two years later he would continue the theme with his 'Myrthen Waltz' to celebrate the nuptials of Victoria and Albert. London seems to have provided a productive setting for Strauss, and on his final trip to the capital, a few months before his death in 1849, he wrote or began the *Frederick Polka*, *Almack's Quadrille*, *March of The Royal Horseguards*, the *Alice Polka* and the *Exeter Polka*. This time he stayed at the Hôtel Versailles which then occupied number 2 Leicester Place, one block east of the Hôtel du Commerce. His complete works were published by his son **Johann Strauss the Younger** who made just one visit to London to conduct over sixty concerts at the Royal Opera House, Covent Garden (**see WC2**).

He had booked rooms at another hotel, in Fleet Street, which he left almost at once deeming them unsatisfactory, with the result that he was taken to court for non-payment and threatened with debtor's prison

- **THE COLISEUM**, St Martin's Lane, (Tube: CHARING CROSS or LEICESTER SQUARE) was designed by **Frank Matcham**, a leading Edwardian architect of music halls and theatres. He also designed the cheerful Shepherd's Bush Empire and the decorative London Palladium, but he really pulled out all the stops with The Coliseum. It cost £300,000 and back in 1904 was far and away the most extravagant and flamboyant lyric theatre ever built in London. In theatre owner and impresario **Sir Oswald Stoll** Matcham had found the ideal client and there was never any doubt that The Coliseum was built to impress... or even alarm. Certainly Stoll and Matcham's plans to top the building with a vast revolving globe caused official concern. It was deemed illegal and in the end Stoll had to settle for a virtual revolving globe, simulating movement by means of flashing electric lights. Inside, the stage had three concentric revolving elements, a feature which was once publicised by staging a horserace in which three animals ran against the direction of the moving sections, to little purpose. The opening week of what was dubbed The People's Palace of Entertainment and Art was an unequivocal success with more than 67,000 people crowding through the doors. Stoll's personal vision was of a theatre where the public could have access to the highest quality entertainment with a theatre choir, a music director and operatic arias performed alongside jugglers, animal acts and grand spectacles. Radically, all the cheapest seats were bookable in advance, an unheard of gesture of social inclusion in Edwardian times. In the 90-odd years since Stoll and Matcham created the Coliseum, it has gone through a number of

There was never any doubt that The Coliseum was built to impress... or even alarm

Radically, all the cheapest seats were bookable in advance, an unheard of gesture of social inclusion in Edwardian times

phases. It was first a variety theatre, and then its classical credentials were established with performances of the Diaghilev ballets in the 1930s. It was a venue for the big American musicals of the 1940s and 1950s and productions staged here included *Annie Get Your Gun*, *Kiss Me Kate* and *Guys and Dolls*. However it was not until the late 1960s that the former Sadler's Wells Opera, nurtured by **Lilian Baylis** (**see Sadler's Wells, EC1**) and now rechristened the English National Opera (ENO), found a permanent home at the Coliseum. Despite the occasional financial disaster and temporary eviction, The ENO remains there, taking ever-longer summer breaks until an extensive refurbishment programme, currently scheduled to be completed in 2004, restores the Coliseum to something of its former glory, exactly one century after its opening.

- The **HOTEL SABLONIÈRE ET PROVENCE**, Leicester Square (Tube: LEICESTER SQUARE) has long since been demolished. Even its exact original location is disputed, although the south side, now occupied by restaurants, a movie theatre and a bank, looks most likely. This, in any case, was the hotel that experienced an early version of the kind of public hysteria that would later attend 20th century pop stars. It happened when **Niccolò Paganini** first visited London in May of 1831. He stayed here until the end of August and the concerts he gave in the intervening three months garnered receipts of over £10,000 and ranked as the most sensational the city had ever seen. Even other musicians were staggered by the virtuosity of his violin playing. **Mary Wollstonecraft Shelley** confided that Paganini "threw her into hysterics". She added that she delighted in "his wild ethereal figure" more than she could express and concluded that the sounds he coaxed from his violin were all "superhuman". No doubt at this point some contemporary kind of paramedics carried her out, swooning. Paganini himself was understandably alarmed whenever he ventured beyond the lobby of the Hotel Sablonière et Provence. "I can never step outdoors," he complained, "without being mobbed by people who, not content with jostling me, actually get in front of me and prevent my moving in any direction, address me in English – of which I don't understand a word – and even feel me to determine if I'm flesh and blood." We can only speculate whether the widow Mary Shelley was one of the mob feeling him up.

Mary Shelley confided that Paganini "threw her into hysterics". She added that she delighted in "his wild ethereal figure" more than she could express